Development Practitioners in Action

Praise for this book

'It has taken us ages to ask the elusive question - *'who is a development practitioner'*? Linje Manyozo has, provokingly, responded. Cogently presented, this is an incredible piece of work, laying bare the subtleties of development discourses. Linje, you are a true development practitioner.'
Jonathan Makuwira, Professor of Development Studies and Deputy Vice Chancellor, Malawi University of Science and Technology

'Nothing is more compelling than a human drama presented in a comedic way. Development practitioners would rather listen and watch than read. But for this book, reading becomes a joyful experience as you encounter the wisdom shaped by honest mistakes and lessons learned.'
Cleofe Torres, Development Communication Practitioner

'In this enlightening book, Linje Manyozo leads us into a voyage from expertise to "human-tise". Combining his passion for people with the praxis of participatory development and his lifelong practice of working and listening to communities, Linje invites development practitioners and experts alike to be in service to the communities they are working for and get involved in a development that as his great-grand mother once said, is felt in the heart.'
Guy Bessette, participatory development researcher

Development Practitioners in Action

Linje Manyozo

**Practical
ACTION
PUBLISHING**

Practical Action Publishing Ltd
25 Albert Street, Rugby,
Warwickshire, CV21 2SG, UK
www.practicalactionpublishing.com

A catalogue record for this book is available from the British Library.
A catalogue record for this book has been requested from the Library of Congress.

ISBN 978-1-78853-215-0 Paperback
ISBN 978-1-78853-214-3 Hardback
ISBN 978-1-78853-216-7 Electronic book

Citation: Manyozo, L., (2023) *Development Practitioners in Action*, Rugby, UK:
Practical Action Publishing, http://doi.org/10.3362/9781788532167.

Since 1974, Practical Action Publishing has published and disseminated
books and information in support of international development work
throughout the world. Practical Action Publishing is a trading name of
Practical Action Publishing Ltd (Company Reg. No. 1159018), the wholly
owned publishing company of Practical Action. Practical Action Publishing
trades only in support of its parent charity objectives and any profits are
covenanted back to Practical Action (Charity Reg. No. 247257,
Group VAT Registration No. 880 9924 76).

Cover design by Aboriginal artist, Juliette Nakamarra Morris from
Yuendumu, Australia
Typeset by vPrompt eServices, India

Contents

Acknowledgements

The truth is, this thing, this remarkable experience that has generated extensive experience and, consequently, a rich body of knowledge, has been a collective endeavour. So, any errors are thus collective, sensibly so.

In the spirit of 'writing with country' as conceived by Martuwarra River of Life and others, I acknowledge that this book was written on both the country of the Wurundjeri, Gunai Kurnai, and the Maravi Kingdom. It was equally co-authored by the rivers, mountains, hills and the valleys, insects, the lizards, the plants and the forests, the goats, the chickens – with all of whom I share equal citizenship of this God's earth.

Starting from the village that raised me, I am indebted to the three wise women: Julita my mother, Lydia my grandmother, and Maria Abiti Bisani my great-grandmother, through whom the world was created and made to make sense for me. Above all, they gave me the tools with which to navigate the turbulence of this life and the systemic violence that characterizes all modes of production on the road to the future.

To beautiful people: Robin Mansell, Nora Quebral, Keyan Tomaselli, Shakuntala Banaji, Claudia Lopes, Mukhwiri Jonathan Makuwira, Stavroula Tsirogianni, Karmen Jobling, Antonio Castillo Rojas, Mufunanji Magalasi, Dovile Soendergaard, Andrew Jaspan, Jo Tacchi, Thomas Tufte and Chrissy Thakwalakwa for shaping my thinking and pedagogy, and, to numerous practitioners and service providers, for colouring my development praxis.

To Professor Cleofe Torres, Guy Bessette, and Trina Mendoza who read the whole manuscript and shared some critical thoughts; and to many friends who read bits and parts and shared feedback. To Heather Elmes and Gillian Bourn and Louise Medland for the painstaking copy-editing and proofreading. Many thanks to Chloe Callan-Foster and Rosanna Denning at Practical Action for guiding me during the book production process. I am forever grateful to Julia Bernado for the many conversations we have had at Meeniyan Art Gallery on and about this work.

To Judy, Sarah, Sophia, and Ben Lawry; Pip and Marie Nicodemski; the late Royalty, Lois Hartley – for helping me and my son to settle in this new place.

And, as always, to my son Benji, an allegro of humanity, a cadence of goodness, a sonata of love, an opera of kindness, who teaches me to count backwards that Shakespearean clock that tells the time.

The cover picture is by Aboriginal artist, Juliette Nakamarra Morris from Yuendumu, just outside Alice Springs in Australia. The Wanakiji Jukurrpa (bush tomato [*Solanum chippendalei*] Dreaming) travels through Yaturlu (near Mount Theo, north of Yuendumu). 'Wanakiji' grows in open spinifex country and is a small, prickly plant with purple flowers that bears green fleshy fruit with many small black seeds. After collecting the fruit the seeds are removed with a small wooden spoon called 'kajalarra'. The fruit then can be eaten raw or threaded onto skewers called 'turlturrpa' and then cooked over a fire. 'Wanakiji' can also be skewered and left to dry. When they are prepared in this way it is called 'turlturrpa' and the fruit can be kept for a long time. In contemporary Warlpiri paintings traditional iconography is used to represent the Jukurrpa, particular sites, and other elements. The Wanakiji Jukurrpa belongs to Napanangka/Napangardi women and Japanangka/ Japangardi men.

Reminding everyone of the shared bonds of humanity that yoke us, as we anxiously await our collective appointment with the future. Meanwhile, we remain faithful to the cause of a world that is democratic, equal, and just. *Semper fidelis*.

About the author

An enthused student of time, Linje Manyozo is a Communication for Development scholar and practitioner based in the College of Design and Social Context at the Royal Melbourne Institute of Technology in Australia. He is formerly the Director of the MSc Programme in Media, Communication and Development at the London School of Economics and Political Science; and a Communication for Development Specialist in international development. Linje is also a Research Associate of the Department of Development Studies of the Nelson Mandela University in South Africa.

This treatise builds on Linje's professional efforts in participatory development practice, and of course his epistemological experience of and with indigenous knowledge. His pedagogy, research, and praxis have centred on strengthening citizen voices and investment thinking as panacea for sustainable development. His contribution to development dialogues appears in the form of books, articles, online videos, and numerous development policies and dialogues.

Prologue

Policy makers are rarely poor: to understand poverty they must study it. A visit to the village promises a glimpse of the real thing, but meeting poor people is not so simple. Anything from fuel prices to bad weather can obscure rural poverty from the urban visitor. Close-typed reports and colourless statistics are the staple diet of the office-bound expert. It is from them that the facts and figures on development come. But it is the occasional day out, the field trip, the visit to the village that offer city dwellers and policy makers their most colourful and enduring images of rural life ...

The brief rural visit, often a guided tour, provides urban outsiders with their only experience of rural poverty ... The visitor sets out late, delayed by last minute business, by subordinates or superiors anxious for decisions, by a family crisis, by a cable or telephone call, by mechanical or administrative problems with vehicles, or by urban traffic jams ... The programme still slips behind schedule ...

Whatever their private feelings, the rural residents put on their best face and receive the visitor hospitably ... Speeches are made. School children sing or clap. Photographs are taken. Buildings, machines, construction works, new crops, exotic animals, the clinic, the school, the new road – all are inspected ...

As the day wears on and heats up, the visitor becomes less inquisitive, asks fewer questions and is finally glad, exhausted and bemused, to retire to the rest house, the host official's residence or back to an urban home or hotel. The village returns to normal, no longer wearing its special face.

When darkness falls and people talk more freely, the visitor is not there.

Shortage of time, the importance of the visitor and the desire for information all influence what is perceived. Lack of time drives out the open-ended question; the visitor imposes meanings through the questions asked. Checking is impossible and lies become accepted as facts. People are neglected while formal actions and physical objects are given attention ...

But above all it is the poorer people who tend to be unseen and remain unmet.

Robert Chambers (1981)

CHAPTER 1

Development practitioners in action

Understanding the development practitioner

In the main, this treatise is a Marxist rejection of what Robert Chambers rightly describes as rural development tourism, a very orthodox method of understanding people and their development needs through choreographed development encounters into and with communities (Chambers, 1981). Perhaps in line with Chambers' rejection of this kind of development approach, numerous students of society conceive a development of the people, one motivated by spirituality and basic needs, and reflective of the multipolarity and the pluriverse nature of our societies today. For a people's development to happen, generating necessary knowledge is critical. It is the reason Robin Mansell (2011) discusses development as the organized production of knowledge, knowledge that shapes any resulting development interventions, hence the contention, 'whose knowledge counts'. The book proposes an antithetical process, one that relies on the leadership of the field-based development practitioner – to inspire people to co-design interventions that are sustainable and which make sense to local people.

Once on a teaching tour in Europe, an enthused development student asked me: *What does a development practitioner look like?* This book, *Development Practitioners in Action,* converses with this question and, of course, Chambers, by examining some of the key attributes, behaviours, and character dispositions of development practitioners. Let me state clearly that I acknowledge that the idea of development could be dead – that the term is ideologically fluid and more of a statistical and economic construct; that there is so much inequality and, as such, life is more 'about survival now, and not progress' (Sachs, 2019). From experience, development is about much more than placing money and resources at the disposal of a people. And, as I explain later, and as Chambers, Escobar, Makuwira, and lots of post-Marxist thinkers and practitioners have demonstrated, development is largely non-monetary – it is spiritual and cultural. Development entails the politicization of the development process, a collaborative process that brings together dissenting and conflicting voices and interests to co-design 'alternative worlds we want to create' (Kothari et al., 2019).

Such development is about locating a people's place in their ecology, in which there is a great coexistence between humans and nature. It is about recognizing the multiverse of people, with different concepts of spirituality and God, the diversity of notions of progress and growth, and the fact that development is not necessarily about financial growth (Kothari et al., 2019;

Martuwarra River of Life et al., 2020). Despite these contradictions and contestations, there is an agreement that whatever development is chosen, at the implementation level, development is mostly shaped by the behaviours of its field practitioners. A farmers' club will certainly improve its fortunes if financial inclusion services are made available and, in tandem, guidance is given by a kind and caring business development advisor. Such mentality and behaviours enable practitioners to effectively co-design and co-create lasting development interventions with and alongside people.

Central to the work of this development practitioner is the ability to see and hear *other* people and ourselves. This practitioner has a sustained relationship with local people and not just through what Robert Chambers conceives as a brief and guided visit – but rather a trusted, research-informed engagement offering cultural symbiotic returns to all parties involved. As such, this book proposes a *pedagogy of seeing*; of empathy and feeling as the foundation stone for capacitating development practitioners to be more humane, compassionate, understanding, and to exercise a certain level of indigenous intelligence beyond their formal training. The offerings herein are rooted in field practices from KwaZulu-Natal to the Kalahari, from Eastern Cape to Lewisham in London, from Nkhata Bay to Maputo, from Kagadi Kibaale to Gippsland and in many experiences of various field staff. It is coloured by practical experiences in public health communication, theatre for development, agricultural extension, rural business development, and participatory action research in which our teams walked rivers and hills in search of people's stories and experiences that could be employed in empowering people.

As quoted in the prologue, Chambers raises concerns with the failure of the urban-oriented expert to *see* and meet the actual poor people. And the reason is that their visit is prescribed and choreographed by a coalition of development organizations, government departments, and local elites. Granted this priori, even if deliberative development emphasizes listening to or involving communities, the first real task of the development practitioners then is to *discover the people*: those left behind by local politics, extreme poverty, project biases, and unrealistic development architecture. What this chapter sets off then is a discussion about this journey – the journey to find people, to meet them, to recognize them, to build trust, and to establish relationships with them – which should occur long before we discuss co-designing development with them. To summarize the book as a question: *How do we prepare and capacitate development practitioners of the field to see and meet people?* This is a variation of the student's question: What does a development practitioner look like?

This work makes a strong argument that the thinking, the researching, the doing, and the operationalization of development from the think-tank to the community is known as the *praxis*. In other words, praxis is the established culture or tradition of implementing theories, ideas, concepts, and policies in development. When we break this down, it leads one to conclude that development praxis comprises five main components or layers: 1) theory and concepts; 2) policies; 3) tools and skills; 4) the political economy of financing institutions; and 5) attitudes and behaviours. Arturo Escobar and other postcolonial theorists have raised questions about the relevance of western and orientalist *development theories and concepts* in responding to the needs of people in the global South.

Policies are actionable interventions and programmes translated by governments and organizations from development research and knowledge. Chambers and others have contributed to the creation of participatory development *guides, tools, and skills* to enable experts to collaboratively design, implement, and evaluate interventions alongside each other. This book interrogates the fifth aspect, concerning attitudes and behaviours. The argument is that one can have these guides, manuals, tools, and skills but without the right spirit, the right emotion, the right behaviour, or the right leadership qualities, we end up with development practitioners with a condescending attitude towards local people and their cultures.

So, who is a *development practitioner*?

Development practitioner is an umbrella term describing all manner of professionals, experts, and field staff who work with communities for a significant period of time, with the aim of improving service delivery, building local resilience, reducing social determinants of health, and increasing socio-economic productivity (NSW Department of Community Services, 2009). Chambers mentions experts who make brief and guided visits to communities. That could be one way of doing development practice, but it does not make one *a development practitioner*, who must have a sustained relationship with a community. What does practice mean? There is a thought structure that assumes that theory and practice lie on opposite ends of the development spectrum. Within this tradition, one will find criticism of academics as lacking or requiring practical experience; in fact, there is a movement of academics who take time off the academy to do some practice, often by taking leave of absence. Because at a certain point in their teaching or research careers, these academics expect to be asked, 'Have you done any development practice?'

Another thought conjecture conceives theory as equivalent to practice; much of the efforts have been invested in practices or efforts that allow for collaborative development programmes. These individuals combine their academic career with some level of practice. For example, one teaches journalism while contributing journalistic pieces to major media outlets, or teaches public health while advising government or institutions on public health projects and programmes.

In both cases, adaptive learning initiatives are being established as part of capacity building. Within these scenarios, participatory learning frameworks are introduced to address specific development goals by bringing together researchers, practitioners, policy makers, and institutions. The recognition is that learning occurs in a praxis, the confluence of theory, policy, and practice.

For this book, however, the notion *practitioner* does not exclusively refer to those who are involved in implementing development interventions on the ground. That would terribly exclude thousands of men and women who might, in the language of Chambers in the *Prologue*, 'be office bound'; yet they richly contribute to the continuum and architecture of development practice. The book defines development practice as a continuum which starts from research and knowledge generation, travels down to the development of policies and best bet practices, then results in the exchange and utilization of knowledge and technology. The aim is always to improve the welfare of the people. Hence, the principal attribute of a practitioner is this ability to translate knowledge.

In this case, an academic doing research on maternal and child health in some locality is a practitioner if their work leads to generation of evidence and knowledge that improves the way an issue is understood. A government decision-maker who reads this research and uses it to develop effective policies for the government or development organization is also a development practitioner. Yes, they are 'office-bound' as defined by Chambers, perhaps with limited understanding of specific and local contexts, but they are practitioners.

The behaviour change communicator who takes this policy and uses it as a guide to prepare and scale out educational media content and programming is very much a development practitioner. And so too, the health surveillance assistant or agriculture extension officer based in the community who visits homes to follow up on adherence to best practices. Or a community art centre manager who helps a marginalized community to increase the market value and research of its local artworks, they too are a development practitioner. Sometimes they are employed by a community or development organization. At times, however, they are just what Gramsci would conceive as an organic intellectual. Someone passionate about local people, their representation, and welfare who works towards improving their livelihoods without expecting anything in return.

This book is about this primary and critical part of development practice. And instead of discussing questions of tools and skills for either entering the community or working with people, this book addresses the question of mentality: *What kind of person should a development practitioner of the field be?*

This discussion introduces and distinguishes two kinds of development practitioners who are not mutually exclusive. The first group is the *development practitioners of the office*, who study poverty and become experts generating research and knowledge that decide policies and strategies. From the perspective of Chambers, these 'office-bound experts' will occasionally conduct rural development tourism, 'the brief rural visit, often a guided tour – that provides urban outsiders with their only experience of rural poverty' (Chambers, 1981). Often, we will find these development practitioners of the office working in high positions in government or development organizations, developing and studying 'close-typed reports and colourless statistics' as they put together policies, strategies, and white papers that will shape development implementation long after they are gone. Christopher Shepperd (1981: 7–8) outlines how these experts have become key to the international development architecture.

> *Many Third World countries are still heavily staffed with expatriates. All are experts ... Speaking to the Minister, calling a top-level meeting, sending black and white officials scurrying, is the leader of the gang – the short-term consultant. Sharp-shooting, hard-talking, high-flying – often he holds the purse strings of an international aid agency or his own government. But a developing country may have only three weeks to prise these strings from his hand. His own purse is well-lined. The white faces behind big desks are expatriate civil servants 'on loan' to the Third World government. They are the aid policemen who make sure money is spent properly. They are the aid itself – a gift of expertise – like a set of encyclopaedias ... Some experts live in villages. Some do their best to focus attention on the plight of the underprivileged.*

But not all these experts should be seen negatively. Shepperd himself discusses the 'good expert' who becomes the 'champion of the poor, shunning luxury, living in a mud hut among the people, heroically exposing exploitation wherever he finds it'. These are the experts who care about the poor and underprivileged, and they 'stand on principle and lose their jobs'. As such, working alone, 'they can never effectively challenge the local structure of power' (Shepperd, 1981: 7–8). Therefore, some of these experts have the best intentions. In fact, Guy Bessette observes in comments to this manuscript, 'Some of them, without the experience or the connection to the field are people of good faith and only need to understand the necessity to be more grounded and humble.

For Shepperd, however, most of these experts are development mediators, 'they are the human interface between the North and the South', and a 'vehicle for perverse and inappropriate values', a point Deborah Eade (2007: 637) would emphasize years later. As observed in the quote above, they are there in workshops and meetings, men and women of importance, with sharp and intimidating memories of places, histories, and nature of development interventions the world over. I have encountered these several times. When they speak, they want everyone to know that an important person is speaking. They have the best templates and guidelines, they are masters of standard operating procedures, they have the widest network of connections through which they just know the 'right' researchers and consultants.

They themselves have been investigators on numerous development studies and projects – they personify development, they breathe development, they smell development. In fact, they are development in themselves. While discussing the prevalence of racism within the development sector, Themrise

Khan (2021) makes a strong point about the colonial and racist structure of the development sector itself. Khan notes that the aid sector tends to look down 'on countries based on their wealth, history and global positioning', emphasizing that 'racism in international development comes from anyone associated with northern agencies, white, black or brown, by virtue of their location in the north and position within the sector as funders, implementers and intermediaries'.

The second group comprises *development practitioners of the field.* They are known by a range of titles: development fieldworkers, field officers, extension officers and managers, social researchers, small medium enterprise development experts, anthropologists, rural financial advisors, community engagement experts, communication for development specialists, participatory development communicators, theatre for development practitioners, health surveillance assistants, community media journalists, forestry officers, natural resource management specialists, gender officers, community volunteers ... the list goes on. Suffice to mention that these two groups are not mutually exclusive. We do have practitioners who have been policy makers, and policy makers who have been practitioners. What is critical is that these specific jobs instrumentalize the person; one begins to function as per institutional requirements of the job.

Much of their work is largely about working with people, and usually very little to do with policy making. Usually, compared to the development practitioners of the office, who have higher degrees and education, development practitioners of the field have usually been trained on the job by other practitioners or by the communities themselves. For example, Cecilia Alfonso and Gloria Morales, originally from Chile, manage the indigenous Warlukurlangu Art Centre in the Northern Territory of Australia. This centre is located in Yuendumu, a small community located about 300 kilometres outside Alice Springs. The cover for this book is a painting by an Aboriginal woman, Juliette Nakamarra Morris, who is affiliated to this art centre.

And as observed by Professor Siobhan McHugh (2018), Cecilia Alfonso and Gloria Morales would not have been considered to be 'the most obvious candidates to negotiate the fraught politics and cultural protocols of a remote Aboriginal community'. Their passion for indigenous art and their quest to advocate for it would evolve over time. McHugh observes, 'Yet, over the past 15 years, their blend of passion and hard-headed pragmatism has transformed the Warlukurlangu Art Centre into one of the most successful in Australia, earning the praise of the Warlpiri artists it supports' (McHugh, 2018).

Just like Alfonso and Morales, development practitioners of the field acquire knowledge of the development sector from engaging with and interacting with local people and the issues at hand, and usually, they have an organic sense of how development challenges can be resolved. In the case of Cecilia Alfonso, such an organic acquisition of the local development scene involves both negotiation and managing tensions. There are times it can be conflictual, but the community will work with a practitioner if they see returns. Alfonso thinks the art she found was, according to McHugh, 'dreary'. McHugh further describes Alfonso's and Morales' recounting of their first encounters: 'She [Alfonso] told the Warlpiri people there was a lot more competition in the market and they'd have to "lift their game". Some in the community were upset. "They thought I was insulting them because I was very blunt", she said.'

They have been good with experimenting with local solutions, yet in many cases, they feel their work is not really appreciated by the urban-based experts and planners. They will sometimes have a diploma or first degree in the arts and development related fields. Whatever the nature of their work, the essence of *development practitioners of the field* remains collaborating with communities in employing participatory action learning methodologies to resolve local development issues. In the case of Alfonso and Morales they took time to learn the local art styles. Of this effort, McHugh (2018) details the history:

> *One of the first things Ms Morales did when she arrived at the art centre was extend the artists' colour palette. In nearby Papunya Tula, the dot painting that kicked off contemporary Aboriginal art in the early '70s had a well-established brand based on traditional ochres in red, yellow, black and white.*
>
> *The Warlukurlangu artists had already distinguished themselves with the use of much brighter colours, but with acrylic paints available in hundreds of colours Ms Morales saw the chance to go even further. After all, the artists showed her the landscape was alive with colour— as one of the foundation artists at Warlukurlangu, Paddy Japaljarri Stewart, was fond of telling her.*
>
> *Paddy showed Gloria the orange of natural honey, the kaleidoscope of colourful flowers after rain, the fluorescent green of the budgerigar. She increased the palette to about 300 colours and the artists took to them with alacrity. One of them was the late Alma Nungarrayi Granites, who painted luminous celestial skies to tell her Seven Sisters story. Gloria gave her seven new shades of blue to extend her range, along with new techniques. 'Before I painted dots. Now I do splatter too,' Alma said.*

At the centre of these interactions are indigenous research methodologies that aim to empower local people, and thus its instruments and tools are rooted in local ways of knowing and looking. For example, some researchers working among the Martuwarra Country in Western Australia have employed a participatory research method of attending which is itself rooted in Aboriginal ontology. In this methodology, there is an outsider-insider 'acknowledgement of the interdependence of all beings', in which it is accepted that 'humans come into being through their relationships with each other and with Country'. As such, the methodology 'emphasises becoming "sensitive, communicative, and alive within a more-than-human, co-constitutive world" where research is a form of creative engagement between Country and Country's human co-authors'. In this case therefore, 'Country is thus a key author and research partner' (Martuwarra River of Life et al., 2020).

For Guy Bessette, development practice of the field, which he conceives as participatory development communication, is about consolidating 'community participation with development initiatives through a strategic utilization of various communication strategies' (Bessette, 2004: 1). Likewise, Freire discusses the role of participatory dialogue in ensuring that outside experts do not end up prescribing strategies and solutions; rather development practice of the field becomes a process of building both consensus and *conscientização* (Freire, 1970: 45, 67). As such, one outstanding attribute of this group of development practitioners is that they are quite engaged. They have a deep thirst for knowledge and understanding of the local development and demographic terrain, and know by heart who locally has the skills, knowledge, and resources to resolve local development questions.

This book lends itself to the second type of development practitioners. I emphasize that there are moments and nuances where these two groups engage in symbiotic relationships, feeding off and building on each other, as they interface with people on the ground. The book, however, is not a manual or guide to how to do development with people. One will find numerous guidelines in the public and private libraries. In fact, in *Involving the Community*, Bessette (2004) provides a comprehensive, step-by-step guide on how best to engage, work with, and involve people in deliberative development processes. He outlines the *roles*, the *methodologies*, and the *tools* for undertaking such initiatives. In this kind of work, there is a great deal of frustration by the practitioners who must deal with limited funding, pressure to complete projects in the shortest time and deliver results under almost impossible situations, hostile power brokers, and so forth.

Likewise, Australia's NSW Department of Community Services (2009) also provides a guide on 'practical tips' on working with Aboriginal communities in delivering empowerment programmes. These 'tips' revolve around actual steps and things a practitioner should do, like studying and consulting local maps, local organizations. At the centre of this work is the wide acknowledgement that these frontline development officers must overcome all these constraints, put a smile on their faces, and work with people to produce results that make sense to policy makers and people on the ground. It is a hugely challenging task.

This book will not duplicate, but rather build on the practical tips and suggestions by Bessette, the NSW Department of Community Services, and other similar guides. It seeks to examine the *philosophical orientation* of these development practitioners. What does a development practitioner or a development field officer look like? For a long time, I approached such questions as matters of field strategy and tactics. I have recommended they read participatory rural appraisal (PRA), rapid rural appraisal, participatory development communication, participatory rural communication appraisal or whatever methodology would come to mind. Yet the question is much more epistemological and of course very personal: *What does a development practitioner or a development field officer look like?* In other words, what are the epistemological, philosophical, and empirical dispositions that enable one to effectively conduct development with people? What this book does therefore is to approach the question like Konstantin Stanislavsky approached the question of method acting in *An Actor Prepares*. Stanislavsky's (1917: 14) key message is about preparing for roles through training the conscious which will eventually 'best prepare the way for the blossoming of the subconscious'.

And which development are we talking about?

A certain kind of twisted thinking has been permeating public discourse in much of the global South, especially in the least developed countries. Usually promoted by party politics, or certain forms of academic analysis, this thinking seems to suggest that the government develops people, and that development is measured by infrastructure and other tangible socio-economic indicators. Such discourse is problematic, especially when assumptions are made along ethnic, racial or regional lines: that one group could prevent another from developing.

Over the years I have had the opportunity to traverse countries and communities as part of my development work. In most of these spaces, one would not find proper clinics, hospitals, schools or other necessary infrastructure to deliver social services. Yet I encountered beautiful enthusiasm from the so-called poor or marginalized people. This enthusiasm exists not just in the agriculture or fishing business, it is in the spirit of daring to explore various economic opportunities. There were those travelling across regional or national boundaries selling or procuring products to sell back home. Others were exporting agricultural products. Around these remote 'underdeveloped' communities, new houses of corrugated iron sheets are being built, and an organized network of informal economy has been germinating and bearing fruits.

A deep pursuit of non-monetary development seems to lie in some of the indigenous communities I have visited. Elderly female artists have begun to experiment with new kinds of fabric painting with dye generated from earthly materials. The young girls living and working in the city have returned home to listen to the old and wise women on what indigenous knowledge is advising in terms of managing their urban-oriented families. Government departments from the urban centres are seeking out indigenous elders on indigenous ways of managing issues such as wildfires and insects attacking commercial crops. Which brings me to the role of not-for-profit organizations and, of course, cooperatives and social enterprises.

In this kind of people's development, the concept and understanding of development are expressed and experienced in concrete terms, existential it might seem. In the Fourth Declaration of the Lacandon Jungle for example, the Zapatista Movement (1996) outlines a new form of people's development that comprises 'necessities' as opposed to the oppressive and powerful forces who seek to:

> take the land so that our feet have nothing to stand on. They want to take our history so that our word and we will be forgotten and die. They do not want Indians. They want us dead. The powerful want our silence. When we were silent, we died, without the word we did not exist. We fight against this loss of memory, against death and for life. We fight the fear of death because we have ceased to exist in memory. When the homeland speaks its Indian heart, it will have dignity and memory.

This concrete development can only be built on the words and worlds of those who are oppressed. As such, development cannot solely be conceived in monetary and economic terms. Rather, development can be conceived as the collective efforts of men and women to use their words to construct a 'plural, tolerant, inclusive, democratic, just, free and new society'. The oppressive classes cannot participate in this process because for the Zapatista Movement (1996), they are just 'the salesmen of the remains of a destroyed country, one devastated by the true subversives and destabilizers: those who govern'. This process of deconstructing the old development paradigm is also a simultaneous process of regeneration, rethinking the future. This process is evidence driven, research informed, and involves dialogue and discourse. Just like Paulo Freire, the Zapatista Movement (1996) believes that this process can only be led by oppressed men and women, after all 'in the world of the powerful there is no space for anyone but themselves and their servants; In the world we want everyone fits' (Zapatista Movement, 1996: Part III). Creating a new future involves, for the Zapatista Movement (1996), a critical participation in transformative discourse:

> Many words walk in the world. Many worlds are made. Many worlds are made for us. There are words and worlds which are lies and injustices. There are words and worlds which are truths and truthful. We make true words. We have been made from true words … In the world we want many worlds to fit. The Nation which we construct is one where all communities and languages fit, where all steps may walk, where all may have laughter, where all may live the dawn. We speak of unity even when we are silent. Softly and gently, we speak the words which find the unity which will embrace us in history, and which will discard the abandonment which confronts and destroys one another. Our word, our song and our cry, is so that the most dead will no longer die. So that we may live fighting, we may live singing.

What this means is that for oppressed peoples, development should be visible in their daily lives, not just statistics in the office-bound expert.

Rural farmers, for example, with the support of digital technology, can now sell their products to better markets at good prices. This is not just a statistic, but a material reality. They can access lifesaving information through SMS, the internet or local radio. Money is sent and received via mobile phones. The school fees can be paid on time, and for someone working in the city, they can send money back home to dependants at the press of a button. Across all these significantly remote and marginalized places, I saw the same fierceness and desire to improve the self, families, and communities. People are on the move. From farming to agribusiness, from smuggling to participating in the hospitality sector, local people seem to have grasped the future with their hands.

It was during my stay in one of these remote communities that I met Nyangwira, a woman whose work involves pleasing travellers or researchers like myself. We spent quite a long time in the week I was in this district talking about the future. After all, Nyangwira educated me, the past should be left behind, and we should focus on where we are headed: the future. She had finished high school back home, located hundreds of miles from this rural town centre, and had come here to work in a restaurant. One thing led to another. The promised job in the restaurant did not materialize and eventually Nyangwira ended up in the situation I found her: entertaining travellers. She had a child who was approaching the end of primary school. After my work assignments, I remained in touch with her.

Over the years, there has been a discourse that these rural and remote regions are 'underdeveloped'. The central argument is that post-independent governments, usually dominated by certain ethnic and business cabals, as feared by many postcolonial thinkers, have marginalized other ethnic and racial groups and regions. This has resulted in a breeding ground for some political conflicts; the allocation of national resources seems to privilege certain regions, races, and tribes. For the minority tribes, their leadership has sometimes argued that federalism is the only constitutional facility for empowering their regions to be responsible for their own development. Fair argument. Yet development cannot be given because it is not something any institution or group can possess.

So, what is development?

There is this widely held assumption that the west is developed, or that the urban parts of the global South are also developed. Much of the discourse and practice of development is shaped by international development organizations, which in turn, borrow much of their development epistemology from western universities and western government departments and arms of international development. The idea is to peddle this assumption, that all peoples of the world, want to, in the words of Daniel Lerner (1958), seek to become like the westerners. Such a development paradigm is linear, economics-centric, and problematic – such that there is a need to think of development outside the western lens, hence the proposed notion of a pluriverse (Kothari et al., 2019).

Nowadays the news is teeming with reports of desperate people attempting or undertaking dangerous journeys from the 'poor' countries to either Europe or North America. After all, many of those immigrants who successfully made similar journeys can send money back home and provide reports of excellent social services especially in health and education. And for those of us who have travelled, we seem to be amazed at the high-rise buildings we find in the west or the urban parts of the global South. A footnote that should not be overlooked is that much of this 'western development' was built on slave labour and resources stolen from the global South. The economic indicators seem to suggest that the west is indeed more developed. Yet are these economic indicators right, or is infrastructure really development?

An elderly woman I met years ago on an academic research trip was hesitant to tell stories to our team, fearing our team would drive away with those valuable stories, then use them to develop foreign places and towns. Or think about my great-grandmother, Abiti Bisani, who in an interview for my BA history research project, conceived an existential development: a development that can be touched, eaten, and felt in the heart; a development that allows people to live close to the graves of their ancestors. It is for this and similar reasons that the country of Bhutan, according to several sources, would conceive an idea for the Gross National Happiness (GNH) index comprising nine indicators: good governance, community vitality, living standards, time use, education, cultural diversity and resilience, and ecological diversity, as well as health and psychological well-being.

Yes, it is true that many of these remote and regional towns and countries might not have the high-rise buildings of Chicago, London, Johannesburg, Rio de Janeiro, Manila or Seoul. Yet far away from these 'developed' places, exists a perspective known as *buen vivir*, which looks at life not from the economically deterministic economic indicators, but from the perspective of harmony – harmony with each other and with nature. In addition to this unique perspective, an abundance of natural resources can be found. Take Lake Malawi, for instance, with its abundance of freshwater – an immense asset that the region hasn't maximally harnessed for irrigation agriculture. The rainforests of Amazon, the Congo or Papua are fantastic economic assets that can fuel the green economy even if they are being besieged by a cabal of corrupt politicians and businesses. The fertile lands of Burkina Faso, Kenya, Peru, Brazil, Viet Nam, Papua New Guinea or Zimbabwe are great capital assets for commercial agriculture.

These regions may seem underdeveloped. They are the future, not the past. The fact that they have not been stained with unplanned urbanization and overpopulation is exactly why they are the greatest resource the world has. In many of these marginalized places, the people here have rarely relied on the central government; in many cases, led by religious institutions, they are driven by the desire to author their own development.

The developed countries and cities may boast high-rise buildings and shopping malls with food stalls on every corner. But they also have the highest rates of homelessness, unemployment, family violence, gun crimes, and lifestyles most poor people cannot afford: Living in houses they will pay for their whole life, only to be repossessed by the lenders and banks when interest rates increase and so too mortgages. Not to be too idealistic, many of these 'underdeveloped' areas harbour their own serious problems, too. They experience high rates of female school dropouts, early marriages, unplanned pregnancies, and health inequalities. Development is thus more about available opportunities and freedoms that enable people to pursue their ideals and dreams, writes Amartya Sen. Yet dreams are much more than aspirations. In indigenous contexts, dreams are associated with appreciation of the spiritual origins of our world (Martuwarra River of Life et al., 2020). In Western Australia for example, *Tjukurrpa* is traditional dreaming. For indigenous country and communities, dreaming as in *Tjukurrpa*, entails that:

> the ancestors created the world and laid down the laws for people's behaviour; [and the] Tjukurrpa refers to origins and powers embodied in country, places, objects, songs and stories. [This Tjukurrpa] is a way of seeing and understanding the world and connects people to country and to each other through shared social and knowledge networks ... Tjukurrpa is the past, but timeless. Tjukurrpa is the present. Certain repeated actions, such as ceremonies, songs or use of ritual objects, affirm a connection to the past. Tjukurrpa is the future. It continues to provide substance and meaning to peoples' lives (Western Australian Museum, 2022).

Development could thus be conceived as that space, that encounter, where the practitioner (in some instances a volunteer) works with local people to participate in dreaming. Development is all about dreaming and appreciating the first law of the land. Likewise, Jonathan Makuwira (2007, 2014) conceives development as the sum of resources, their potential and capacities that people and communities must have to improve their lives. While governments can ease these processes, it is the people who can develop themselves. Thence development is not manifested in the material things we can have, but in the stories, freedoms, and non-material assets which make life amenable to the majority.

Several rivers, winters, and moons ago, my part-time lover/friend Nyangwira texted me. '*Alongosi* (my brother), the kid finished high school and I am sending him to university.' This is real development, in all its glory of potential and capability. Development is this insistence by the current generation to invest in the future generations so that they can achieve social mobility, no matter the challenges. Development is about the sacrifices the present makes to push the future into accessing credit lines of a new social mobility.

Development is not about the things we do not have now. It is not even about this notion of 'having'. It is about the collectivity of experiencing this new social mobility – even if it may be out of reach today, we hold on to the belief that it will be in reach tomorrow. We hold on to the belief that when the sun rises in the morning, men and women will, in partnership, be standing on the foothills of the rising sun, waiting for their appointment with the future.

Capacity building of development practitioners

Capacity building is not merely a technical jargon for training. Within the development context, its earliest use is associated with human rights-centred approaches. Deborah Eade (2007) traces its intellectual and political roots to the liberation theology of the Catholic Church in Latin America, through Freire's critical pedagogy, postcolonial feminism, and more recently, in participatory development literature and practice. In the process, capacity building has become a buzzword of international and community development practice. Eade (2007: 632), however, warns that for most western institutions, the concept is being flagged in relation to western liberal interest in scaling down the state's ability to intervene in people's lives, including providing safety nets, which has usually involved the privatization of public services, and the emphasis on good governance, and democratization.

When it emerged within the leftist political thinking and practice, capacity building was always about contending with competing interests in development, and, for Eade (2007: 632), the role of the outsider was to 'support the capacity of local people to determine their own values and priorities'. In this instance, value was placed on local experiences and experimentation. Yet over the years, as development has become more of an industry and spectacle, organizations have found themselves facing pressure to deliver results in the shortest time possible. They are expected to demonstrate long-term benefits of their interventions even after their programmes cease to enjoy aid. As such, the notion of capacity building has come to take centre stage in development practice, granted that focus is on sustaining the interventions after funding has ceased and external expertise has left. Scholar Jonathan Makuwira argues that in development, any organization or institution that claims to build capacity would be making assumptions that are serious in the way development is conceived and implemented. For Makuwira, three assumptions exist about this discourse of capacity building.

The first is that organizations and institutions assume that it is they that have the technical expertise and knowledge of development. In fact, Eade (2007: 633) observes that development literature often assumes that 'capacity building is an exclusively Southern "need", and that international NGOs are among those best placed to meet it', yet 'they do not have any inherent capacity to build' such capacities. In this case, Makuwira (2007, 2014) identifies capacity building with institutional or bottom-up processes that develop competencies and capabilities in the south. As such, capacity building could be driven by institutional interests or could be driven by local agendas. When driven by organizational agendas, capacity building comprises factors that are 'intellectual, organisational, social, political, cultural, representational, material, technical, practical, or financial' (Eade, 2007: 633). When driven by grassroots interests, capacity building becomes the process and strategy of 'enabling those out on the margins to represent and defend their interests more effectively, not only within their own immediate contexts but also globally'.

The second assumption highlighted by Makuwira is that knowledge is a commodity, a thing, just like development itself, and as such, it must be passed on from the knowledge centres to those who do not have it. Nevertheless, there is so much the north and its institutions can learn from the south. The danger with this assumption is that NGOs do have the capacity, yet for Makuwira (2007, 2014), the failure of many development interventions demonstrates that such NGOs lack capacity. Worse still, the spectre of relationships between the north and the south occur within the framework of linear transfer of financial and technical resources, in which for Eade (2007: 635), 'hard' resources are transferred in return for 'soft' resources in the form of information, 'stories', and imagery used for advocacy and fundraising. This relationship is driven and controlled by money. The pressure to achieve observable results in the shortest time becomes huge. Thence, 'aid agencies are always in a hurry' as they feel pressured 'to spend in order to justify their existence to their constituencies and to their donors'. In the end, after capacity building workshops have been organized and the participants have provided 'positive feedback on their evaluation forms, and so capacity has been built', one finds that 'a year later, there is nothing to show for it' (Eade, 2007: 637).

The third assumption concerns the footnoting of experience and experimentation by the people who live through the actual challenge; and the consequence is that, usually, local and indigenous knowledge are often disregarded when it comes to discussing capacitation. In fact, what it means is that capacitation can only occur within established or orthodox structures, such as classrooms, workshops, or formal training sessions where capacity can be built. The further implication is that such building of capacity can be measured scientifically in terms of what Cadiz and Dagli (2010) describe as 'learning gains'. Yet there are fruitful partnership arrangements that can be built with the support of local organic intellectuals. For Eade (2007), even if aid limits the quality of local development that can be implemented, it is possible to use aid resources to build long-lasting capacity building interventions. In this case, capacity building is about 'solidarity-based partnerships' that develop organically through interactions with the local partners (Eade, 2007: 637).

This book seeks to explore two main forms of building capacity. The first is the orthodox approach, associated with formal education, in which development or community development students attend universities and colleges in order to attain formal qualifications. The second concerns the training-learning model in which capacity building partnerships engage in adaptive learning using participatory and action learning strategies. These approaches should not be seen in isolation. Often, people who have undergone formal training in development or international development make effective contributions to the adaptive learning approaches. As such, these two approaches should be seen to be in a symbiotic relationship. Yet the question remains: What attributes does such capacity building aim to produce in the development practitioners of the field?

The development practitioner of the field

The philosophical orientation of a development practitioner is a subject Freire himself has paid close attention to. He describes development practitioners of the field as revolutionary leaders, revolutionary educators, or dialogical and problem-posing teacher-students. These practitioners are about recreating.

Freire recognizes that the pedagogy of the oppressed, of which participatory development is one component, requires facilitators who can co-create development democratically using 'critical and liberating dialogue' (Freire, 1970: 65). For this to happen, these development practitioners must be sincere, authentic, and humanist educators in a 'pedagogy of humankind' that is itself a liberating praxis (Freire, 1970: 54). So, what are the behavioural and philosophical orientations of this educator? Freire (1970: 89–92) explains thus:

> *Founding itself upon love, humility, and faith, dialogue becomes a horizontal relationship ... Dialogue cannot exist, however, in the absence of a profound love for the world and for people. The naming of the world, which is an act of creation and re-creation, is not possible if it is not infused with love ... Dialogue cannot exist without humility. The naming of the world, through which people constantly re-create that world, cannot be an act of arrogance ... Dialogue further requires an intense faith in humankind, faith in their power to make and remake, to create and re-create, faith in their vocation to be more fully human ... Finally, true dialogue cannot exist unless the dialoguers engage in critical thinking.*

These four attributes – love, humility, faith, and critical thinking – formulate the preliminary basis for this book. And then I have added another notion, leadership. All these become philosophical characters that should ideally be reflected in our development practitioners of the field. In my development work, I have often encountered participatory development experts who treat people with disdain; they are arrogant, rude, condescending, and full of self-aggrandisement. These are people who bring chairs to local communities or talk to people while standing, because they cannot imagine sitting down in the sand with people to dialogue on issues and problems as equals. When we bring all these four attributes together, what we have is the praxis of listening.

This treatise proposes a pedagogy of seeing as the foundation stone for training development practitioners to be more humane, compassionate, understanding, and liberated alongside providing them with new technical knowledge, skills, and tools. Chambers (1981) argues that development policy makers are less likely to be poor themselves, thus their understanding of poverty depends on their ability to study it. His argument is that the real poor people remain 'unseen and unmet' largely because of logistical, technical, and typographical challenges.

Eventually, once the development visitor goes back to their hotel, 'the village returns to normal, no longer wearing its special face', and eventually, people begin to 'talk more freely' (Chambers, 1981). This chapter propounds a *pedagogy of seeing* as a pathway towards building a world view in fieldworkers to enable them to cultivate lasting relationships so as to enable people to talk more freely. What this book advances therefore are frameworks for building within development practitioners the wisdom of the people atop their formal training. The people's wisdom contributes to the opening of a practitioner's heart to see and feel those they are working with.

Going back to our question: *What does a development practitioner or a development field officer look like?* This book draws on Antonio Gramsci's notion of *Concezione del Mondo* popularly translated as 'Conceptions of the World' which, Joel Wainwright (2010) defines as 'things that inform our understanding of the world and our place in it', and each conception is 'inherently practical and philosophical, relational and political'. This chapter propounds a *practical* development fieldworker *mentality* that guides social relations during the design and implementation of interventions at the local level. Whereas this practical mentality might pre-exist before entering the field, *it happens* in the process of executing development. This means that the social relations between the fieldworker and the communities are generated in action; that is, during development practice.

The father of liberation theology, Gustavo Gutiérrez (1971), introduces and describes a form of pastoral practice known as 'preferential option for the poor'. This entails a strong ideological, epistemological, and practical orientation of not just considering the perspective of marginalized groups but adopting a progressive willingness to tolerate and embrace what historian Thompson (1963) conceives as history from below. The fundamental and critical aspect of doing participatory development involves acquiring the *attitude, constitution, and skills* to live and engage with people. *Doing* development at the local level is largely a matter of being able to find and meet these people; people who are different, people who think differently, who speak differently, who smell different, and whose concept of time and space is different.

Development practice of the field then becomes pastoral practice for exercising the *preferential option for the poor*. It is about celebrating the multiplicity of voices and the alternative ways of knowing which lie outside our familiar epistemological trajectories. In this case, development practice becomes a spiritual vocation, because it requires students of the human condition to acquire this *preferential option for the poor*. It is thus a question of inclination, bias towards, and love for people. To be a successful development fieldworker, practitioners must have genuine love for people. They must have fallen in love with people and their dreams.

This sits in contrast to the dominant syntax of development practice of the office. Here orthodox education and its instrumentalist pedagogy become a cog in what Bertrand Russell (1935/2004) describes as the 'cult of efficiency', where the significance of knowledge is based on its economic benefits. The graduates from such programmes understand the theories and manuals that allow them to appreciate the 'tyranny of work' (Russell, 1935/2004: 3) required to be an orthodox development worker or scholar. This book acknowledges that formal development training emphasizes curriculum and pedagogy that produce 'work-ready' graduates. Yet there is a growing epistemological realization that much decision-making in the field largely depends on emotional intelligence, virtues, and values – the very preferential option for the poor. Ideally, liberatory development education provides a greater sense of humanity, compassion, and love, becomes a vehicle for critical thinking, and a platform for adaptive leadership training.[1]

Modern tertiary education is being informed by results-driven educational systems that prioritize generating specific skills and outcomes. This also implies the increased presence of the industry in the classroom, which then shapes the content and pedagogy. Yet the classroom, which would have been an ideal public sphere for cultivating an epistemological renaissance, is facing several challenges: curriculum standardization, ambiguous pedagogical expectations, dictatorship of prescribed curricula, managerialism of tertiary education, and high costs of higher education which often exclude children from lower socio-economic backgrounds.

The result is Freire's *prescriptive* education, which regulates the way the world is explained to students. This book proffers a different *kind of teaching* that touts listening and love as major graduate attributes, with a focus on developing emotional intelligence. In this way, practitioners can be more humane, more compassionate, and more tolerant towards others. A central feature of this pedagogy is compassion, which Kristin Neff (2015) describes as the ability to clearly see, feel, and recognize suffering, especially of others.

Discovering the poor people

One pressing conundrum that Chambers poses in the prologue concerns the visibility of poor people to policy makers. Chambers outlines the biases that make it hard to see and meet people: first is that visitors usually 'come from urban areas; they want to find something out; and they are short of time'. The second bias is that 'the visitor sets out late, delayed by last minute emergencies', and as a result 'the programme slips behind schedule'. The third reason, as observed by Chambers (1981) concerns the fact that the visitor is 'encapsulated' by their transportation, government and local elite, and passability of roads. The fourth is that even the selected rural people put on a performance, 'their best face' to 'receive the visitor hospitably', ensuring they respond as expected to 'bring benefits and avoid penalties'.

As such, development practitioners of the field must transform the nature of their work so that they will meet and see the people that matter, being able to listen to them and collaboratively co-design deliberative development with and alongside them. For this to happen, these practitioners should cultivate requisite abilities and capacities to discover and listen to people. So, what does discover people mean?

Firstly, discovering the people implies contesting the 'close-typed reports and colourless statistics' and instead going out and meeting people in their own communities. As much as research is vital in helping us to understand people and groups, there is something valuable in sitting and consulting real people about the issues affecting them – especially through a visit that is not controlled by the local development industry. This is critical because official reports have sometimes reflected the tendency to be orientalist and biased. On 21 June 2006, an Australian Broadcasting Corporation (ABC) *Lateline* bulletin featured a segment, 'Sex slavery reported in indigenous communities'. This segment was preceded by a series of sensational clips and interviews with 'experts' that revealed cases of sexual abuse in indigenous communities in the Northern Territory. The *National Indigenous Times* journalist Chris Graham (2017) observes that following this, the *Lateline* team, intensified the sensational reports centred on the community of Mutitjulu.

In the immediate aftermath, the Northern Territory Government (2007) instituted a Board of Inquiry into the Protection of Aboriginal Children. The result was the *Little Children Are Sacred* Report. This would lead into the Emergency Intervention in June 2007, whose focus, scope, and approach on indigenous communities would later be seen to have been misplaced, considering that even the NT Government Report itself cautioned that the problems of sexual abuse 'do not just relate to Aboriginal communities' (NT Government, 2007: 3). As such, any interventions to address these challenges should acknowledge the structural violence and the 'breakdown of Aboriginal culture and society', and that, 'a determined, coordinated effort to break the cycle and provide the necessary strength, power and appropriate support and services to local communities, so they can lead themselves out of the malaise' (NT Government, 2007: 12–13). It was thus emphasized that people can only develop themselves.

Secondly, development practitioners of the field should seek alternative research. In the case of the NT Government Report, the writers might argue their report was objective, that it did not call for the Emergency Intervention, and in a way distance themselves from the interpretations drawn from their work (NITV, 2017; ABC News, 2017). Yet evidence seems to suggest that the Report emphasizes the 'extreme urgency' of government intervention (NT Government, 2007: 5–6, 12), treats Aboriginal people with very colonial stereotypes of violence, drunkenness, and indigenous community disintegration. Yet critically, the Report seems to ignore other reports into the same problems carried out by reputable indigenous organizations and scholars. It ignored several other expert reports from Aboriginal groups.

Scholars (such as Professors Judy Atkinson and Boni Robertson) and organizations (such as Top End Women's Legal Service, the defunct Aboriginal and Torres Strait Islander Commission, ATSIC) were footnoted and marginalized. In fact, the abolishment of ATSIC in 2005 left indigenous communities without state or federal level representation in government policy formulation (Graham, 2017). In this case, Marx's observation about the subaltern not being able to represent themselves seems real: 'They cannot represent themselves', he illustrated (Marx, 1852/2010: 62). By getting rid of an indigenous representation body, for Marx, the Aboriginal communities were made to become 'incapable of asserting their class interest in their own name'. Resultantly, the Emergency Intervention lacking the legitimacy of local support and ownership would cause grief in indigenous communities.

Years after the failed intervention itself, a study led by the University of Sydney and the Menzies School of Health Research established that 'there were significant drops in school attendance and the birth weight of babies' (Higgins and Brennan, 2017). It seemed like the report duplicated some of the key observations from the *Lateline* coverage. Likewise, several journalists have exposed the specific problems with the testimony presented in the *Lateline* programme (Graham, 2017). So how do development practitioners discover and work with the people?

A pedagogy of seeing

This pedagogy of seeing is fundamentally one of love and refers to both the pedagogical approach of the teachers and the pedagogical outcomes of those education systems. Artist Janelle Monáe (2018) discusses love as a transformative force that 'has the power to change the world'. In the same vein, *Huffington Post* contributor Ivette Dubiel (2016) links love to education by arguing that teachers should demonstrate that they care for and love their students beyond the classroom, and that they want them to 'flourish'. Similarly, this treatise builds on such *pastoral practices* of teachers who care beyond the classroom. For example, Principal Akbar Cook of Westside High School in Newark, New Jersey, is one among many (The Ellen Show, 2018). He realized that most of his students came from broken homes and were experiencing homelessness, often wearing dirty clothes, which bred bullying, fighting, and absenteeism. Cook resolved to bring washers and dryers to the school, creating a laundry facility as a way of *taking care* of that obstacle. It was an initiative that made students realize Cook *was more than a teacher*; students considered Cook a person who 'had your back' and who loved them (The Ellen Show, 2018). For development training, this is the kind of pedagogy that builds a sense of humanity in our students so that they attain the right epistemological and empirical constitution to fall in love with people beyond the classroom.

How then do we train development practitioners to co-design development with and alongside people with love? Certain encounters initially set the ball rolling for this book.

The first encounter comes from my own interactions with students whom I have taught over the years, who have asked me what I would recommend if they are to pursue development practice as a career. The second encounter emerges from my international development work, where I encountered educated but out of touch policy makers, making me wonder if there could have been a pedagogical intervention during their studies to teach them to be more human and understanding. The third encounter emerged after the 2008 global financial crisis, when some UK students, à la Post-Crash Economics Society (2014), began lobbying western universities to diversify the economics curriculum in terms of its ideological underpinnings, content, and perspectives. The fourth encounter concerns the impact of rapid modernization and urbanization, severely interrupting social lives, pushing people to cities, where there is increasing unemployment, loneliness, and alienation. Think about Joyce Carol Vincent, a beautiful 38-year-old woman, discovered in 2006 lying dead on her sofa in a north London apartment – three years after her death (Morley, 2011).

Such a context calls for a different kind of pedagogy. A pedagogy that not only aims to produce development practitioners with the necessary knowledge and skills, but rather, is a *pedagogy of seeing*, in which emphasis is on showing our development students that there is this thing, this force that is going to change the way they see themselves and others. It is about capacitating development practitioners to fall in love with people and encouraging these practitioners to appreciate listening as a facility for transforming communities and societies. This is also a *pedagogy of feeling*, whose praxis involves building adaptive leadership skills in development practitioners to serve others. Freire (1970: 89) himself saw critical pedagogy as a form of revolution whose oil was the practice of love itself, noting, 'the naming of the world, which is an act of creation and re-creation, is not possible if it is not infused with love'. How does this kind of pedagogy register within the restrictive confines of formal education and prescribed curriculum?

The engaged educator

The first pathway is through an engaged educator, in this case, trainers and teachers of development subjects. Freire spells out this teacher of critical pedagogy in contrast to the banking educator. A clear power imbalance exists between the banking educator and the student, largely because 'the teacher knows everything and the students know nothing' (Freire, 1970: 73). In critical pedagogy, however, Freire's problem-posing educator aims to challenge students to intervene in their social reality. Students become co-curators of the educational experience. Yet there is more to this democratic and radical approach to education. It is about the behaviour and the values of teachers, and the extent to which they are dedicated to their students and their world. For Gutiérrez, there is no difference between teaching and pastoral practice. In many traditional settings, a teacher and a preacher are known as *mfundisi*: to teach is to deliver pastoral care.

What this means is that such a critically engaged teacher becomes an interested party in the welfare of their students. This teacher is Antonio Gramsci's organic intellectual. Some of these organic intellectual teachers may have grown up in the neighbourhoods in which they are teaching, or they may have come from similar socio-economic backgrounds; nevertheless they embrace their new homes and students. In the same vein, bell hooks (1994: 3) discusses the transformative teachers who know the students, 'the parents, economic status, what the students' homes look like and the experiences in the homes'.

Speaking to PBS NewsHour, Nadia Lopez, principal of an underprivileged Brooklyn school, argues for an adoption of a pedagogy that responds to the empirical reality of violence and marginalization in which students find themselves. For Lopez, one major approach to get teachers to become engaged involves participatory mapping of the local housing developments, thereby helping the teachers to understand the challenges that they need to address in the classroom. In a segment on PBS NewsHour (2016), Lopez observes:

> *One of the things that I do with my teachers is to walk them around the community for them to see what we are up against every single day. My teachers were able to see it from the ground, by us walking through the housing development, and seeing for themselves, the lack of employment, the lack of resources, so many young men who are on the streets at 12 or 1 in the afternoon, who are doing nothing. This is drawing our kids every single day, so when they leave us at 2:30 or 3:00 in the afternoon, that's all they know. They hang out on the streets and they have no other purpose ... We have to start engaging in the solutions.*

The implication of what Lopez is elucidating here is that development cannot be taught out of context. The teacher's prime motivation should be the love they have for their students. A deep-felt and genuine love would mean that instead of providing the education in the classroom and then concluding 'it's time that you go home', teachers are telling students, '*Caminhamos lado a lado*' (we are going to walk together side by side). In that respect, this pedagogy is a journey that the teacher and the student take together. Such an engaged educator is not just the 'smart book professor' that bell hooks (1994) criticizes, but one who goes beyond the prescribed curriculum by showing their students the consciousness of time. For Principal Lopez, such engaged pedagogy involves either bringing the outside world into the classroom or literally taking the students out to observe and learn from their own immediate world (PBS NewsHour, 2016).

Similarly, one South Side Chicago teacher, Kadir, emphasizes that a teacher is there not simply to deliver the curricula, but to motivate the kids 'because they do not believe in themselves' since 'inspiration is not there in the house' (VPRO Metropolis, 2014). What this means is that teachers ought to pursue additional intellectual curiosities such as learning students' backgrounds, empowering and inspiring them via personalized guidance, and educating them on the consequences of poor decisions. What is clear from these duties is that teaching is not merely an exercise in transmitting knowledge. Rather, teaching is a revolutionary process of shaping the world view of students to become rounded individuals critically engaged with the key questions facing our world today. To do this, teachers should learn their students' names, cultures, where they come from, and then listen to their life stories.

The magic of words

The second pathway through which a pedagogy of seeing can be delivered is the power of storytelling, the strength of speech, and the magic of words. This ensures that students are inspired by knowledge, but at the same time, are made to understand that 'the classroom should be an exciting place, never boring' (hooks, 1994: 7). This is so because language enables us to explain things, allowing us to define and represent the world. In language, teachers can find building blocks for creating colourful mental pictures that will stay with students for a long time. There are many ways of doing this. How do teachers do this?

One way is to develop a narrative or style of speaking that allows us to cater to the hearts of students. As teachers we can practise our delivery. Language is not just about the way we deliver our discursive representations – it is a culmination of our soul, a harvesting of our emotions, our spirit, our personality, and our character. Our way of speaking provides a window into our deep thoughts and character. No matter how engaged a teacher might be, no matter how knowledgeable about their subject they might be, if they are seen to be impersonal, uncommunicative, unkind, condescending, or self-centred, then their ability to deliver effectively will be hampered. For hooks (1994), it should also be remembered that an interesting teacher's teaching style becomes the base upon which most students will build their pedagogical approaches when they become teachers in the future (yet most students would not want to emulate the teaching styles of their teachers). What this chapter is advocating is not just a teacher who is good at effectively delivering the content, but one who cultivates interesting ways of using language to empower students to love themselves, the world, and other people.

During my second year of high school in the seminary, I had a wonderful teacher: a priest who taught mathematics. There were moments during these classes when he would pick up a 'worldly' novel he was reading in his spare time and read sections of the book to us. Here was a man who had taken the vow of celibacy lowering his voice to read us pages from Truman Capote's collection *Music for Chameleons*, for example. This was utterly enchanting for us students, cultivating within us a love for knowledge and a fascination with the magic of words. I can still hear the priest's deep and husky voice as he read to us about this aristocratic woman who played Mozart on her piano for the chameleons who seemed to love the music. In between there is a conversation about the history of Martinique itself and its relationship to colonial France, an imagination that fed into our thirst for French as a language.

Growing up in Malawi in the 1980s under severe poverty and under a terrible dictatorship, inspirational figures were scarce. What it did for most of us students, was to make us always look forward to having this teacher around. Mathematics grew more interesting and would become a favourite subject that I would later ace in my A levels. So too English, which cultivated in me a love of Shakespeare, Dickens, Langston Hughes, Lorraine Hansberry, Abioseh Nicol, Anton Chekhov, Leo Tolstoy, Henrik Ibsen, Ngũgĩ wa Thiong'o, and several other authors that would enable me to experience the new and strange geographical horizons beyond the confines of the dictatorship under which I was reared. The magic of words led me to love literature, which then enabled me to love mathematics.

There was something in the voice of this teacher that drew us students close to him. It fused us with his passion for books and the way he saw the world. In the spoken and written word, I found love for colour and smell. In reading any book, I would always wonder what the writer of the lines was seeing in their mind or smelling at the time they were writing the book. Reading a book therefore became a fascination with discovering the author, because I believed by doing so, I could then do justice to the book. This experience would also inculcate in me the love for libraries and bookshops. A teacher's ability to use the right words will go a long way towards ensuring that students love the subject, but also treasure the classroom as a preparatory launchpad for life. *Learning no longer remains a burden but an enjoyable experience.*

For some students, they come to school with little inspiration. It therefore falls on the teacher to motivate them to love the subject at hand, but also challenge them to understand why this class is fundamental to their being able to play a transformative role in society. In using words to paint magical realism in the hearts of students, the engaged teacher masters the understanding of the science of its frame, its dreams, and its smells. The colour of words encompasses the respect that is accorded to the intention and spirit of the words. I have learnt about the power and smell of words from three women who raised me: my mother, grandmother, and great-grandmother. These women have always had a way with words. It was in their words that we children were made to discover the world, to learn its secrets, to construct and deconstruct its gender, to discover its possibilities. It was in and through the colour of their words that we would embark on voyages of epistemological discovery, to discover the world itself. As such, words have the power to open gateways and worlds of possibility for students who are seeking answers, but do not know where to find them.

Development practice as leadership

As explored in Chapter 6, the third pathway through which this pedagogy is delivered is through exposing development practitioners to leadership opportunities and personalities. This will reveal how, within the confines of people's worlds, development practitioners can exercise leadership while transforming spaces. Leadership does not necessarily have to be a subject in tertiary institutions for students to be exposed to its principles. It should be mainstreamed in whichever courses they are taking. What are we talking about when we say leadership? And when it comes to development practice, leadership in what?

It is becoming increasingly realistic that community spaces are becoming culturally diverse. Groups from different cultural and socio-economic backgrounds are finding themselves sharing the same space. This raises challenges of speaking across cultures and social classes. The classroom then becomes that training ground that should build in these development students the ability to work and engage with others who are different from them: those who look different, speak with different accents, and those with different social orientations. Bessette (2004: 8–9) discusses this leadership attribute as a type of 'attitude you adopt in interacting with community members, the way you understand and discuss issues, the way you collect and share information', and the way in which one 'establishes communication with people'.

Thus, such a leadership *attitude* centres on the ability to understand group and community dynamics. This brings up the necessity of group work, even if an increasing number of assessment requirements seem to be bent towards examinations and gauging individual excellence. Yet it does not stop the engaged teacher from using group work in teaching the students. This offers the space for students to not only establish conflicts but also resolve them. At the same time, students who are high performers have the opportunity to help those laggards who struggle to understand new knowledge and concepts. Thompson (1963) discusses the notion of 'diffusion of literacy' to explain how working-class groups would teach themselves how to read and write. Thus, horizontal education allows for the bottom-up development of adaptive leadership.

Leadership is the ability to inspire others to work towards positively trans-forming the world around us. It is an exercise in collective efforts, and of celebrating other people's skills and knowledge. Instead of feeling threatened by them, we harness them for the benefit of the greater good. A critical component of engaged pedagogy would identify industry leaders in certain fields or topics and bring them into the classroom to both teach and inspire our students to see how such knowledge is benefiting the world. There are increased cases of teachers in many schools and colleges taking students on learning excursions, and there are cases in universities where students are involved in organizing various work-integrated learning.

Building leadership training into prescribed courses and curricula allows students to appreciate the power of decision-making and how it affects both the process and the quality of the end-product. They also learn the significance of taking and sharing responsibility, and how the disruptive behaviour of one or two individuals can ruin the efforts of the team. Group work teaches them to know others, their strengths and weaknesses, training them to be empathetic and understanding. These things take a long time to cultivate; there are frustrations, tantrums, and short tempers along the way. Yet what it builds in our students is the realization and appreciation that other people's feelings, skills, and perspectives matter – and that notwithstanding how right they feel about their opinions, it is important to listen empathetically to others.

Chapters in this book

This book contains seven chapters, and addresses one fundamental question: *What does a development practitioner or a development field officer look like?* This first chapter discusses 'Capacitating development practitioners' through a *pedagogy of seeing,* as the foundation stone for training aspiring development practitioners to be more humane, compassionate, understanding, and liberated. Such a practical mentality empowers them to discover and fall in love with the people. Beyond providing development practitioners with new technical knowledge, skills, and tools, *pedagogy of seeing* is itself an epistemological manifesto of how development fieldworkers cultivate lasting and transformative relationships with local people.

The second chapter 'Teacher, teach us to see' engages with the indigenous notion of *seeing,* particularly the epistemological idea of being able to make sense of complex phenomena. It explores the role of a development studies teacher in providing a liberating pedagogy that *awakens* the students. This allows the classroom to be transformed into a performative space for honing development studies students' tools and skills, enabling them to be awake to the world around them. The chapter argues that for students of society – development practitioners especially – their ability to make sense of the world depends on their ability to seek and understand other ways of knowing.

The third chapter, 'On empathy for the other', explores the question of *pedagogy of feeling.* Here, critical pedagogy utilizes liminal spaces to train participants in acquiring multiple perspectives as they seek to co-design a world that is equal, democratic, and just. An effective development practitioner should not be merely a depository of development knowledge and prescribed curriculum. It maintains that for development practitioners to become more rounded, they must learn to *feel* with the other. Teaching students to feel for and with the other is a foundation of an engaged development field officer.

The fourth chapter 'On women in development' is a continuation of a conversation with classic and modern philosophers, with a particular spotlight on the tenuous relationship between western and southern feminism. The subject of women is of paramount significance in the times we live in: a period marked by increased cases of violence against women, socio-economic exclusion, plus the #MeToo and other radical rights-based movements advocating for increased visibility and inclusion of women. The chapter challenges development practitioners on how best to question whether quintessential equality can be realized in the age of religious and cultural diversity. The chapter expects development practitioners to familiarize themselves with feminist thinking and practices to better handle these issues in deliberative development.

The fifth chapter 'On forgiveness and trauma' is a conversation with South African actor and activist John Kani and the liberation theologian Archbishop Desmond Tutu, who make critical observations about the pain, the difficulties of forgiving, and the complexity of oppression. How does a development practitioner work within spaces where people have suffered so much, brutalized by oppressive systems? The discussion attempts to offer insight into how development practitioners can understand and practise forgiveness as they work with communities who have been antagonistic towards each other. The discussion asserts that marginalized communities have experienced trauma, and that understanding forgiveness allows the development practitioner to navigate the tricky terrain of community consultation.

The sixth chapter introduces the indigenous notion of '*utsogoleri*' as a form of development leadership. It seeks to demonstrate that unlike the development tourist who is a policy maker, the development practitioner of the field exercises leadership during the design and implementation of development interventions on the ground. What this chapter does then, is to provide a preliminary exploration of how leadership in development is manifested, not in the behaviour and work of the policy maker, who has delegated authority (*ulamuliro*), but rather in the kindness, understanding, and tolerance exhibited by the development practitioner of the field.

The seventh chapter 'Wisdom of water' is a progressive teacher's manifesto, inviting students of the human condition to development practice. This chapter proposes that beyond formal development training, field-workers should be imbued with the wisdom of the people. The discussion builds on conceptions of indigenous knowledge to generate five key lessons for development field practitioners in their quest to contribute to the construction and shaping of what Gramsci (1932) described as historical inventory. The chapter builds on auto-ethnographic experiences of growing up in abject poverty and marginalization, of going through the education system where, with the help of teachers of critical pedagogy, I was able to find my own pedagogical voice and style.

Note

1. I am greatly indebted to Julia Bernardo of Gippsland, Australia, for the many conversations we have shared on this topic during our volunteer sessions at the Meeniyan Art Gallery.

CHAPTER 2

Teacher, teach us to *see*

The pedagogy of seeing

The title of this chapter is inspired by Fela Kuti's 1980s classic song, 'Teacher Don't Teach Me Nonsense'. The chapter engages with the pedagogy of *seeing*, especially within the context of development studies teaching. It explores the role of a development studies teacher in providing an education that *awakens* the development practitioner student. This enables the classroom to be transformed into a performative space for developing the tools and skills to enable these future practitioners to *see* the world in its multiplicity and complexity. Students of society should understand that their ability to make sense of the world depends on their ability to seek alternative perspectives and speak alongside people who are different. The chapter addresses two perspectives: the perspective of the teacher, and the perspective of the learner, because both are crucial to the achievement of this *pedagogy of seeing*.

The reasons for writing this chapter are threefold: The first comes from one summer afternoon, when I was having lunch in central London with a group of master's students. Our conversations turned to critical issues facing our modern world. Needless to say, the question of colonialism came up. With enthused urgency, the students identified and vehemently criticized modern-day examples of colonialism and imperialism, covering a range of issues, such as military intervention, trade imbalances, corporate tax avoidance or the theft of mineral resources from the south. They made it clear that they would, with the privilege of their western university education, resist and reject any forms of colonial or imperialistic development projects.

Later that evening, I reflected on those conversations, and in the process thought about our lunch – particularly the cuisine. Our lunch that afternoon had been diverse: pumpkins, squash, couscous, fish, pineapples, tomatoes, onions, cinnamon, coriander, and several other food items imported into the country. Right there in front of us was a teaching opportunity that I had missed. Where do these foods come from? How are they grown, and by who? How are they transported? What marketing and trade systems bring these to the UK and Europe? How much do the farmers who grow these food crops make? How would the students protest against imperialistic or colonial trade practices in ways that would not result in harming the producers on the ground? Did we realize that we were sitting on wooden chairs probably made from deforestation products in the global South?

Is it possible that the shrimp could have come from southern commercial farmers where smaller producers have been pushed away? The content for education had been right there in front of me the whole time. We just could not *see* it: that colonialism was on our plates. That we were eating colonialism itself. It is this idea of *seeing* that this chapter analyses as a central feature of critical pedagogy. In the timeless essay, 'In Front of Your Nose', George Orwell borrows Bertrand Russell's (1935/2004) notion of 'habit of the mind' and defines it as that consistent practice that involves 'ignoring facts which are obvious and unalterable', resulting in our failure to *see* things in front of our nose (Orwell, 1946). This chapter argues that by empowering our students to *see things* from a different perspective, that is, with a 'view from there', they will be able to search and find knowledge in the empirical world around them. And they will too, significantly, know the cause of things – 'Felix, qui potuit rerum cognoscere causas', as articulated by Virgil in the epic poem, *Georgics*.

This brings us to the second rationale, which comes from my own interactions with students to whom I have taught communication and development the world over. During one of the seminars, one student walked up to me and asked about my teaching methods and pedagogy, which they declared had increased their thirst for knowledge. But then they added a request: *Could you please teach us to see the world, to see things, to feel things?* This student was unaware they were taking me back to Plato, Aristotle, and classical questions in education. They were inadvertently asking for a kind of pedagogy that would awaken students, to enable them to see the world, to see things ... and that is not necessarily the same as being woke. Within African American and Pan-African knowledge substructure, *woke* sounds like an *ideological frame of reference* built on a particular experience and understanding of colonialism, imperialism, and racism.

This chapter and of course this book attempt to respond to the student's request by problematizing this transformative pedagogy of listening; an education that liberates students to *see* and *feel*. The kind of seeing I want to believe the student was calling for is not a physiological act of having sight of an object. It is rather an historical and political process of consciousness building that allows and empowers individuals and groups to rise above their own orthodox perceptions, values, and prejudices. As a consequence, they begin to see the world from different perspectives. An education that allows them to break free from the epistemological position of 'the view from here'.

The third rationale concerns the growing disquiet with certain forms of ideological correctness. Certain conversations are becoming almost impossible because discussing particular topics is becoming sensitive, intolerable, or unconscionable. We live in a world where it seems everyone feels they are a victim, resulting in cacophonies of sensitivities we must tiptoe around. In fact, just to bring up certain issues in question for discussion often results in accusations of racism, harassment or cultural intolerance. A growing public culture of concern on social media involves those who consider themselves 'woke' increasingly becoming thought police, humiliating people, shutting down conversations, and accusing others of various forms of marginalization. Concerned about this discursive intolerance, former president of the US Barack Obama criticized this modern culture of 'calling out', which emphasizes the idea of being pure, non-compromising, and judgemental. Obama observed that the 'world is messy, with ambiguities', and as such, grey nuances exist (Rueb and Taylor, 2019). So the question is, how do we *see* and explain phenomena in ways that bring others along with us?

The idea of being woke

With contested origins including the role played by Marcus Garvey, the term 'woke' has its roots in African American polity, especially civil and labour rights advocacy. It is a concept becoming generally used and accepted to refer to the deepening class consciousness (Wikipedia, n.d.). In her album, *New Amerykah Part One* (2008), Erykah Badu examines the significant question of socio-political consciousness in an unequal world. A key strategy for confronting such inequality for Badu is a deliberate strategic programme that ensures people understand the root causes of their oppression, hence the need to 'stay woke'. Badu sings that as she 'searches to find a beautiful world', she will try to 'stay awake'.

In my native Chichewa language, 'to be woke' can be loosely translated as either *kuona* (to see or to refuse to slumber), or *kuchangamuka* (being smart, aware, well-read), or kupenya (to literally open one's eyes), and these three hold slightly different meanings, albeit significant. The first is *kuona* – literally both an act of seeing and also refusing to sleep – which involves seeing itself and making sense of what we are looking at. The second and third refer to the ability to empower oneself with knowledge, and thus imply both *kupenya* and *kuchangamuka*: the state of using knowledge to help oneself and others to understand things better. This entails the creativity to discover, to search for, and to understand new and deep things about our world, and to be awake, which empowers us to be liberated. A rice farmer in a rural area who has information about various markets and rice prices will be on the lookout for unscrupulous business folks, who want to cheat other farmers of their rice by buying it at cheap prices. This farmer who exercises *kupenya* and *kuchangamuka* will negotiate and be able to challenge the businesspeople, asserting that the local farmers will find other beneficial markets. There is thus, in being able to see, a sense of social justice not just for oneself, but for the collective. It is not meant to be a discourse of vindictiveness.

It is this particular application of being woke as a process of acquiring holistic knowledge to improve people's lives that this treatise and this particular chapter is all about. This is an empathetic and imaginative journey that students of society undertake in order to explore available possibilities before making any decision. In this kind of education, students and teachers collectively raise critical questions: 1) Who are we as a people?

2) Where are we going? And 3) how do we ensure no one is left behind on this journey? What we are trying to do is not a matter of mechanics of running a class, but rather to ensure a kind of presence, a kind of *awakening* that should govern the praxis of delivering an enlightenment pedagogy, a pedagogy of seeing, a pedagogy of love. This is a pedagogy that is in an epistemological frequency with reality and the needs and aspirations of the participants.

This book thus aims to fan the fires of a humanist approach to pedagogy, not as a way of confronting the extant ideological *miseducation* and knowledge commodification-driven forms of education, but instead as a way of developing the tools and skills of our students so they can achieve *kuchangamuka:* that state of being awake that enables them to *see*. What this book demonstrates is that this struggle to forge a *beautiful* future that is free, equal, and just requires the necessary step of self-examination and conscientization. The message from Badu was that the denigrating conditions people are living through should provide enough fodder for them to examine their own oppressive conditions; that their own poverty and inequality are in themselves a classroom that should motivate this searching – not for the truth, but for a consciousness that will keep everyone awake. This is her vision for a new America. This is the new pedagogy of *seeing*.

The world has more than one centre

Teachers of critical pedagogy should first and foremost challenge their students to realize that the world has more than one centre. The curriculum content, the prescribed books, the language of pedagogy, and even the group assignments should be carefully planned to ensure that the process and content is ideologically and culturally inclusive. Yet there is also more to the appreciation of a multipolar world – it is an epistemological question. In the aftermath of 11 September 2001, the 2008 financial crash, and, more recently, increased popular support for right wing politics, legitimate questions are being raised as to how we should, as students of the human condition, make sense of history. Instead of blaming poor people for being ignorant and racist in voting against establishments, as students of society we need to ask questions about the lack of morality in neoliberal politics, which may have led people to support right wing causes in the first place. The late American public intellectual, James Baldwin, was equally critical of neoliberal and leftist politics and humanism, which had huge implications for how we write, study, and teach history today.

In a 1986 speech to the National Press Association, Baldwin (1986) conceived the notion of 'view from here' as a form of rigid political perspective that makes it impossible to *see* other people and their history. Building on this concept, the chapter appraises when and how teachers of critical pedagogy can help students achieve critical political consciousness or what Erykah

Badu partially conceived as 'being woke' – but a kind of wokeness that is humanistic, inclusive, and multi-accentual. Yet from Baldwin's perspective, it is imperative that such political consciousness not be informed by this 'view from here', but instead ensure that students have the relevant tools and skills for examining society from the other side.

More than any time in history, students are today consuming and engaging with mass media through traditional and digital platforms. A critical issue that teachers must help students understand is media literacy. Our ability to make sense of the world does not necessarily depend on the objectivity and truthfulness of journalism, it depends on acquiring media literacy – literacy in how the media works and constructs reality and truth, as well as in the ability to seek alternative perspectives. Many news media platforms have been captured by ideological and financial interests. As a result, when we watch news nowadays, we are not watching the truth. Rather, we see carefully selected elements aimed at presenting a certain picture of the world that is shaped by a *view from here*.

In essence, truth is ideological, hence it is a political construction. This makes it even harder for our students to 'stay woke' (to borrow Erykah Badu's concept), because the very concept of woke is a product of certain historical and ideological conditions. Being woke in the western world can mean being unwoke in some places from the global South. This chapter therefore is an entry point into critical thinking for students of society, to give them the necessary tools for doubting and questioning this 'truth'. It argues that dominant neoliberal voices within mainstream media and universities have perpetuated Baldwin's *view from here* as if it is the only and unproblematic frame of reference.

Baldwin's argument seems to complement a thought shared by Said in the revised Foreword to *Orientalism*. Writing in the aftermath of the 11 September 2001 attacks, Said (1978) calls for a deliberate intellectual investment in under-standing other cultures and peoples, for the sake of increasing and enriching our comprehension of the world, others, and ourselves. What this means is that there should be a deliberate effort to celebrate what the philosopher Mikhail Bakhtin (1984) conceived as the *heteroglossia*, or multiplicity of voices, theories, and discourses. In rejection of the American sociologist Daniel Lerner's (1958: 38) observation that 'what the west is, the east seeks to become', this chapter places at its centre the multiple localities that celebrate the experiences, stories, and knowledge of the other. A kind of empathetic social inquiry. After all, the very nature of the classroom is changing; increasingly, it is becoming multipolar, multicultural, multi-accentual.

Likewise, the Kenyan writer Ngũgĩ wa Thiong'o (1986) describes these phenomena as 'moving the centre', the appreciation of a multipolar world. The debate surrounding the role of the classroom in getting students to deconstruct the 'view from here' has grown in prominence in the aftermath of the 2008 financial crisis. A group of economics students at the University of Manchester would establish the Post-Crash Economics Society (PCES).

The PCES (2014) raised fundamental questions about the ability of graduates to deal with real life economics problems, the relevance of the economics curricula the world over, and the need for a radical rethink of the economics syllabi in western universities. The main argument was that the economics teaching and curriculum were lacking any relevance to the real world (PCES, 2014).

As observed by the PCES, traditional training programmes have largely been built on neoclassical economics theories and paradigms. As a consequence, the alternative ways of seeing, reflecting, and analysing the world are hidden from students, thereby denying them the opportunity to acquire a holistic understanding. For students being taught these paradigms and models, they are not provided theoretical antidotes; if they are taught any alternatives, the teaching is often stripped of its historical context, depoliticized, and executed in a way that obscures the underlying assumptions and critical frameworks (Manyozo, 2017). In whichever case, the PCES students are concerned with how symbolic power is contributing to the miseducation of social science students.

A corollary is that such training prevents the student from acquiring a holistic understanding of the world and renders their training irrelevant in other parts of the world. They are thus denied the acquisition of analytical tools with which to, in the words of Freire (1970), speak and unspeak the world. The PCES also notes that students and professors alike have been unable to explain the factors leading to the financial crisis on the basis of their research (PCES, 2014). This might be partly attributable to professors with little or no industry experience; academics with little or no understanding of the world of the other; and the commodification of education leading to competition for high fee-paying students, especially in the fields of finance and economics.

Pedagogy of seeing is therefore an intellectual space for amplifying and celebrating difference. In banking education, class conversations are often structured in ways that intellectually exclude and leave behind students who do not understand this view from here. That is the dominant syntax. Students find themselves in familiar classrooms yet continue to face unfamiliar epistemological structures that marginalize them. What this book is proposing is that students should be present as human beings and as cultural subjects in the material they are studying. It is the reason Freire (1970) observes that education should start from *here* to get *there*. This 'here' implies the *view from there*, that is, their own lives, experiences, and material world which they should learn to define and deconstruct.

In 'Unlearning the myth of American innocence', Suzy Hansen (2017) examines the impact of ideology in the education system, the world around her, and her upbringing that made her become ignorant of her whiteness, her privileged background, and America's oppression of other countries. It was a professional visit to Turkey that made her truly 'see', to such an extent she 'began to *feel* that the entire foundation of my consciousness was a lie'. Where did this lie come from? It comes from a system that Erykah Badu describes as 'Master Teacher', one that puts people to sleep. Hansen (2017) herself describes this 'Master Teacher' education:

> We were all patriotic, but I can't even conceive of what else we could have been, because our entire experience was domestic, interior, American. Our goals remained local: homecoming queen, state champs, a scholarship to Trenton State, barbecues in the backyard. The lone Asian kid in our class studied hard and went to Berkeley; the Indian went to Yale. Black people never came to Wall. The world was white, Christian; the world was us ... We did not study world maps, because international geography, as a subject, had been phased out of many state curriculums long before. There was no sense of the US being one country on a planet of many countries. Even the Soviet Union seemed something more like the Death Star – flying overhead, ready to laser us to smithereens – than a country with people in it.

If the trip to Turkey allowed Hansen to unlearn the 'lie' she had been brought up on, it also exposed her to the way education systematically *unteaches* students, anaesthetizing them from reading the world and themselves to the extent where they cannot *see*. The connections between the educational and social systems are vital in envisaging an education that transgresses, empowers, and results in self-actualization (hooks, 1994).

The view from the other side

Another approach through which pedagogy of love can teach students to see is by challenging them to appreciate the *view from there*. Writing in the *London Times Supplement* of 1966, Edward Palmer Thompson propounded the notion of people's history, as a form of historical reconstruction that requires scholars to read, unpack, and appreciate historical events from the perspective of nonpersons. In and through *The Making of the English Working Class*, Thompson (1963) cemented the notion of history from below as a major scholarly tradition. He noted in the Preface to this timeless classic that even if the subaltern groups live what might appear to be backward, uncivilized, traditional, and 'deluded' lives, they nevertheless 'lived through these times of acute social disturbances, and we did not' (Thompson, 1963: 12). Thompson then proposed 'rescuing' subaltern experiences.

In emphasizing the quest to 'rescue', Thompson was not undermining the popular agency to historical construction. What he was calling for was beyond a new history that represented views and experiences of the underclass. Thompson was calling for a new kind of witness, one who should reject this *view from here*. What comprises this one-sided perspective of history described by Baldwin as constituting the *view from here*?

For Baldwin, the concept of 'here' comprises knowledge and cultural industries that are seemingly neoliberal yet are becoming increasingly hostile and intolerant to alternative viewpoints and perspectives. These industries and their discourses seem to assume what Chimamanda Ngozi Adichie (2009) defined as a 'single story' when it comes to conceptualizing social events and crises and are not necessarily motivated by 'rescuing' the marginalized groups and their perspectives, but rather to achieve certain ideological objectives. Responding to criticism levelled against her for arguing gender is about experiences – and as such, transgender women (who were initially raised as men) have different experiences from women raised as women – Chimamanda Adichie introduces the notion of 'language orthodoxy'.

Language orthodoxy has seemingly morphed into cancel culture – where in our public culture, a hegemony of narrative has emerged within ideological groups on both the right and the left, appearing to have become intolerant of commentariat and punditry that denies difference in opinions. In the process, this discursive carnivalesque insists, 'that unless you want to use the exact language, I want you to use, I will not listen to what you're saying' (Kean, 2017). Adichie argues that anyone associated with leftist politics is expected to 'participate in [it], and when you don't there's a kind of backlash that gets very personal and very hostile and closed to debate'. Adichie is thus rejecting the single-story approach, or Baldwin's *view from here*. There are three aspects to Baldwin's conceptualization that comprise such an epistemological position and perspective.

The first is that because of what he perceives as the existential existence of a shallow sense of sincerity, to an extent, immaturity has become a significant virtue in Western polity. Even as he spoke before the age of social media, Baldwin (1986) seemed to foretell this western fascination with an 'adoration of innocence, this adoration of immaturity'. The tolerance of outrageous thoughts even when they reflect stupidity and immaturity, is considered a great American virtue. For Baldwin, there is a perpetuation of a false sense of sincerity about the well-meaning nature of the system that is complicit in the destruction of lives without acknowledging it (Baldwin 1963: 17). The consequence is that the 'authors of devastation' are also 'innocent'. This is because the system absolves the 'innocent and well-meaning people' of authoring or perpetuating the dehumanizing conditions that the underclass find themselves in and are expected to accept as natural.

The second aspect to Baldwin's notion of *view from here* concerns the deliberate manipulation of memory in which history becomes irrelevant, and thus there is a deliberate denial of what actually happened. Years later, another American philosopher, Harry Frankfurt (1988), would define this cynical nihilistic disregard and lack of respect for the truth as 'bullshit'. Baldwin (1986) observes that the American society has been 'afflicted by this aversion to history', in which 'history is not something you read about in the book; history is not even the past; it's the present'. A good case of aversion to and disregard for history is manifested in popular representations, which are in themselves the 'compulsive set of images that come out of a history that we always deny'.

The third aspect of Baldwin's *view from here* is the growing replacement of history with myths that perpetuate made up realities. He alludes to the violent process of slavery that was dehumanizing and traumatic for the slaves and their families. He observes 'In the effort to deny whence we came; we have had to make a series of myths about it; and myths cannot replace reality' (Baldwin, 1986).

So, what comprises the 'here'?

While Baldwin's criticism was primarily targeted at the politically correct neoliberal thinkers and establishment in the US, his thinking has profoundly contributed to the undermining of western humanism as facing a moral crisis, because in its neoliberal form, history remains unkind to the subaltern. This is what pedagogy of love should bring to students. In essence *the view from here* does not only entail and assume we are all standing in the same place, but that we see the same things, use the same language to describe the same thing, and, most crucially, feel the same things – a kind of globalization of feeling. In a way the *view from here* is equally a hegemony of feeling. Challenging our students to teach fellow students about where they come from would be a great point of departure, but such critical pedagogy should go beyond that – build seminars and tutorials on these stories and narratives, so that students begin to see themselves in the content of their own education.

Essentially, the 'here' is also a liminal space that comprises a political economy of institutions, structures, and vocabularies that, considered together, 'has become a system of reality, a system of ideas, a system of thought, which makes reality very hard to reach, and one that cannot bear the weight of reality' (Baldwin, 1986). Thence, the *view from here* could be construed as the conservative and neoliberal discursive superstructure employed in 'spitting on, defining, describing and limiting' the lives and conditions of the subaltern (Baldwin, 1963: 35). This has implications for critical pedagogy today.

Even with the increased availability of critical theorists, educators and teachers have the moral responsibility to curate the learning environment and also employ alternative theories and perspectives. What Baldwin is pointing out is that there is a kind of critical theory that has in itself become dominant, a purveyor of Adichie's 'language orthodoxy' in which there is an emphasis on a homogeneity and hegemony of seeing and feeling. It has become imperative for example to assume that the experiences of black people in the US are considered, within some civil rights movements, to be the experiences of black people in and beyond the US. It was considered unfathomable for the Anglo-American left to see black people supporting and voting for Trump because he is thought to have said racist things about minorities. The idea of black people having different opinions could not be imagined, because in the world of the *view from here*, every black person should feel the same towards certain people.

Baldwin (1963) himself proposes a pedagogy of love: 'what was the point, the purpose of my salvation, if it did not permit me to behave with love towards others, no matter how they behaved towards me?' To exhibit this love, writers, artists, and thinkers must embrace the 'sensuality' of vocabulary; that is to 'respect and rejoice in the force of life, of life itself, and to be present in all that one does, from the effort of loving to the breaking of bread' (Baldwin, 1963: 53). Again, this has implications for the teaching and learning outcomes in critical pedagogy. Teaching and learning should aim, as articulated by other liberatory and revolutionary educators, to achieve empowerment and self-actualization for both the teachers and the students.

Horizontal learning as learner's perspective

It is often assumed that the success of critical pedagogy rests entirely on the shoulders of the educator. To an extent, yes. What this chapter seeks to do at this point is to emphasize that the learner too has a huge part to play. One major way through which learners of critical pedagogy can contribute to their own awakening is through questioning dominant views, destabilizing them, until they are flushed out of their discursive habitation. The learner has the moral and political obligation to subject such master narratives to constant doubt and undermine its underlying assumptions. In response to this chapter, Guy Bessette observes the need to emphasize the role of what he terms *training-learning*, an organized kind of on-the-job training outside the educational system. He argues, 'In my experience, the greatest educational process for development practitioners resides in continuous social learning, where, following a cycle of action research, participants share with others their reflection on the actions they have been involved with.'[1]

Training-learning has become a key feature of international development programmes, where northern institutions forge partnerships and arrangements that will transfer and build local skills and knowledge. For UNICEF, for example, the Learning Lab initiative has involved the organization working with its implementing partners to share technical knowledge, tools, and skills in relation to social and behaviour change. The organization is involved in financing, planning, and executing the plan of action. Yet it is argued that the Learning Lab is in a way, a relatively 'horizontal capacitation experience in that local implementing institutions and development organisations are involved in sharing experiences and best practices relating to efficient ways of implementing policies in practice' (Manyozo et al., 2020). The overall objective is to consolidate and establish a 'culture of continued learning and experimentation' which would strengthen their capacity to engage with communities in a proactive, participatory way, and to harness new communication technologies in order to scale up and accelerate development efforts (Manyozo et al., 2020).

In a similar vein to the Learning Lab initiative, the Isang Bagsak initiative in South Asia would be introduced as a form of adaptive learning. Describing learning as a knowledge enterprise, Celeste Cadiz and Winifredo Dagli (2010) introduce the notion of adaptive learning as a form of capacity building outside the classroom. They observe, 'adaptive learning is based on the premise that learning from their experiences empowers participants to respond more effectively to new uncertainties, enabling them to change old ways of doing things and allowing them to make better decisions in managing the natural resource base'. In this context, learning takes place through collaborative platforms and processes in which practitioners, researchers, and selected members of community groups come together to co-create shared development experiences.

One such example is the Isang Bagsak learning programme in community-based natural resource management (CBNRM) in Asia, coordinated by development partners and institutions.[2] The aim has been to enhance the practices and approaches in CBNRM. The Isang Bagsak intervention has undergone a number of phases since being pioneered by the International Development Research Centre of Canada in the early 2000s. These phases involved bringing together development communication experts and CBNRM practitioners from Africa and South-East Asia. As such, Isang Bagsak has undergone 'remarkable evolution' by expanding 'from a small pilot project to a multi-organizational community of practice' (Cadiz and Dagli, 2010).

Much of the learning framework draws on the Freirean pedagogical principles of action learning – learning by doing, and largely guided by the ethos of participatory development communication as laid out by Bessette. The Isang Bagsak adaptive learning process comprises four main components drawn from Bessette's (2004) conceptual model in participatory development communication: Assessment, Diagnosis, Planning and Intervention/Experimentation. Using these four frameworks, the Isang Bagsak CBNRM learning model then generated 13 steps by expanding Bessette's model which was considered 'linear' and 'limiting' (Cadiz and Dagli, 2010). These 13 steps would then be grouped in four clusters, namely: building relationships, gaining understanding, facilitating movement, and finally, grounding implementation. So, what did this 'open learning' process comprise? Cadiz and Dagli (2010: 63) highlight the key processes involved in this adaptive learning initiative:

> In terms of methods, the Isang Bagsak project used a combination of the following approaches: 1. An introductory workshop for the in-house team. 2. Team discussion meetings. 3. Direct field application of new principles and practices learned. 4. A regional electronic forum where team discussion highlights for each PDC [participatory development communication] step or theme were posted in separate folders to exchange with other teams in the region. 5. A regional mid-term training workshop. 6. A final regional evaluation and planning workshop. To this cycle of learning and sharing, programme facilitators added monitoring and evaluation activities as well as a component to cap the learning process

by documenting the participating teams' insights and experiences and sharing them with others.

What these learning processes set out to achieve in combination was to challenge learning groups to collaboratively generate, manage, translate, exchange, and utilize knowledge and best-bet practices emerging from their ongoing CBNRM research-based interventions. The fluidity and flexibility of the learning groups meant that the process of generating, exchanging, and utilizing knowledge was very horizontal and participatory, and ensured a mixture of expertise, knowledge, and skills. Both Cadiz and Dagli acknowledge that though the 'learning gains' do take time and are often self-reported, the Isang Bagsak initiative demonstrated a considerable level of strengthening the CBNRM theoretical and practical capacities of participants. Yet the most revealing observation concerns not only the learning gained by a group, but their ability to contribute to the learning process. Cadiz and Dagli (2010: 72) emphasize that 'some learning groups may have increased their knowledge and skills, but unless they bring this new expertise into the cycle of praxis, the change in their behaviour does not meet the goal of the programme'.

What this Isang Bagsak example shows is that horizontal learning empowers the collective student to become their own teacher in the learning process. Through the critical operations of building relationships, gaining understanding, facilitating movement, and grounding implementation, participants are able to build the collective capacity of all learning partici-pants by effectively contributing to this 'cycle of praxis'. In this process the learning gains are also reflected in the way this adaptive learning model allows for the development and experimentation with new theories and practices.

For Professor Cleofe Torres of the University of the Philippines, what Isang Bagsak and similar adaptive learning models achieve is the development of an education that offers a view from there. In an email response to this manuscript, Torres raises questions about adaptive and participatory learning:

But how do we operationalize it? Perhaps the explanation given by Robert Chambers I came across years ago and which I asked our artist to draw might help clarify how the process goes [referring to a drawing of a farmer and an extension worker].Here, both the development worker (extension worker/oppressor) and the farmer (oppressed) engage in the process of rediscovering. They learn to empathise and see how the other sees the world from there. And as their relationship goes longer and deeper, they reach a point where each (without them knowing) liberates himself from the old stance and begins to embrace the view of the other. Its beauty is that it becomes liberating for both the oppressor and the oppressed, and not just one of the actors in development.[3]

It is therefore this ability to collaboratively develop new theory and practices, to allow for nuances and experimentation, and to effectively contribute to the building of the cycle of praxis, that engenders participatory learning as a key form of pedagogy of *seeing*. Such a pedagogical approach empowers learning participants to question and doubt the nature, content, and relevance of text book knowledge generated off-site, and cultivate egalitarian learning spaces that contend with expert-driven knowledge, or what Christopher Shepperd describes as 'wisdom from above' – and then offer opportunities for co-curating knowledge and practices for use by the participants themselves. What this discussion therefore is emphasizing is that any learning practice should empower learning participants to question Shepperd's *wisdom from above* or Baldwin's *view from here*. There are some suggestions on how best to approach these issues.

Development practitioners are not the only experts

With modernization followed by the increased involvement of international and transnational development organizations, we see an emphasis of this omnipresent and omnipotent expert who knows everything – the *development practitioner of the office*; this is the expert who espouses the theology of theory is practice, and who comes into a local context, defines problems and prescribes solutions. It is this aspect that the ABC *Lateline* and Northern Territory Government Report seemed to have failed to appreciate – that it is impossible to study problems in a community without paying attention to the people themselves. This is what Freire conceives as prescription.

Freire talks about a liberatory educator, one who opens up their eyes and ears in order to understand the 'other' story or the other experience. In this case, listening becomes a form of tolerance, which is a duty on our part as development practitioners. There is a tendency among experts to assume that they are the voice of God. They are present at conferences, where they will be the first and last to speak, ensuring their thoughts are adopted as resolutions. Even when questions are raised regarding the local context and the need to consider endogenous factors, these experts will offer complex explanations of how they dealt with similar situations in other countries and contexts. Theories and models that do not exactly make sense will be introduced and thrust down people's throats, with the expectation that they employ these new strategies.

Each society or community has its own throw-away, those left behind, and those hidden from public polity. It could be the caste system in India, the child and slave labour in Asia and Africa, or undocumented immigrant workers in the west. These are groups that fly under the radar, but still experience socio-economic turbulence. As such, they too determine the nature and direction of history. It is not the official story we are looking for – it is the untold story that we should uncover. For example, globally, concerns have been raised about how mainstream media report on minority issues. Historian Cheryl Ware (2017) observes that in Australia, as early as the mid-1980s, the so-called gay press featured 'gay men's personal accounts of living with

HIV or AIDS', in which editors 'utilised individuals' accounts of living with the illness to challenge mainstream media representations of gay men's physical and emotional demise in the "final stages" of the debilitating illness'. Publishing the stories in outlets such as *OutRage* provided these editors with the opportunity to personally contest the uninformed mainstream representations that carried what Ware describes as 'demonising portrayals' (Ware, 2017: 478). The editors became AIDS activists in themselves. Journalism became a site of radical communication intervention considering that most established institutions, especially the church, taught that AIDS is a death sentence. Concerns with mainstream media's representations of minority groups linger on.

When we consider the perspectives of marginalized communities, it allows them to contribute to what Mahmood Mamdani (2007) considers the 'naming' of the problem as distinct from the official and orthodox analyses. In the process, development practitioners are able to participate in the discovery of the people and the writing of history from below (Burke, 2009: 12). It is for this reason that the Australian gay press would, in the 1980s, feature 'individuals' accounts to present the message that it was possible to live, and live well, after receiving a positive diagnosis', keeping in mind there were still medical grey areas and uncertainties in these early days (Ware, 2017: 480).

Acknowledging our ignorance and accepting we are not experts provides a space for a horizontal form of listening with others. This involves development practitioners stepping out of their empirical and intellectual comfort zones of theories and models and humbly subjecting themselves to intellectual scrutiny from others so as to gauge the validity of their knowledge. That is the ethical and political duty Freire refers to: to humble ourselves and enter into dialogue with others about our methods and practices and be able to admit where we are wrong and humbly seek the correction and advice of others – often from people with less educational qualifications or even class status than ourselves.

The virtue of listening

Another major pathway through which learners can contribute to the pedagogy of *seeing* is through the exercise of listening. Within and outside orthodox education there exists a growing establishment of a *view from here*, comprising groups of Twitterati academics and intellectuals, who are angry, teaching this anger to their students, inculcating this spirit of resistance. Some are fascinated by appearing at certain demonstrations or protests against perceived enemies and establishments. There is a growing turn to rudeness, arrogance, and insults in our public culture (Taylor, 2020), because it seems that the more insulting one is towards perceived 'enemies' – particularly the authorities – the more intelligent or progressive one appears to be. Such a growing and dangerous trend nowadays is eating up serious journalism and academy, where journalists and academics, operating from this epistemological pedestal known as the *view from here*, exercise and engage in condescending, derogatory, and sometimes paternalistic vocabulary that lacks historical and critical depth, as a form of performing sincerity and simple-mindedness (Scott, 2020). Listening should become a critical component of critical pedagogy. What is listening? What tools and skills do graduate students need to facilitate listening? How do we measure whether a listening endeavour has worked?

In the aftermath of the Emergency Intervention, for example, indigenous leaders, scholars, and communities would stand up in unison to question the interpretation of the report, the sensationalist media reports, and the irrelevance of the intervention itself (NITV, 2017). The involvement of minority groups and alternative media in contesting mainstream representations helps us to speak alongside these marginalized groups. Such discursive contestations can be theoretically located within critical traditions, such as the work of Assia Djebar (1992) or Gayatri Spivak (1988), both of whom advance various notions of history from below.

Djebar (1992) concerns herself with how French colonialism has been responsible for producing a specialized, subjective, and colonial discourse about the other as exemplified by orientalist Eugene Delacroix's painting, 'Women of Algiers in Their Apartment'. This is a painting generated by Delacroix after visiting Algeria for a few days. He did not even talk to the women in question. A similar orientalist approach by colonial authorities is deconstructed by Spivak (1988) in her analysis of a 1920s suicide by a young Indian woman, Bhuvaneswari.The suicide is undertaken when she is menstruating and Spivak's analysis demonstrates that Bhuvaneswari constructs a political text of resistance using her body. What it shows therefore is that undermining colonial oppression does not necessarily always have to be collective.

In the final analysis, Spivak argues that the female subaltern cannot be heard nor read. What it means is that the subaltern has been speaking but we have not taken time to listen to them. Listening to these voices amplifies the subaltern voices, thus, listening (for us) becomes a form of speaking (for the other). As observed by Gutiérrez (1971), genuine listening manifests itself as a form of speaking for and on behalf of the oppressed. But this is only possible if a critical educator establishes friendship with those they educate, which provides an 'authentic commitment to liberation because love exists only among equals'.

This analysis seeks to demonstrate that listening is a politically conscious decision to enter into a communion with other people. Listening allows us to, in Freire's (1996a) words, 'discover the rich possibility of doing things and learning things with different people'. What this implies is that our faith moves us to be tolerant to other ideas, perspectives, and ways of looking at the world, even if we strongly disagree with them. As such, listening is not naivety – it is a celebration of our recognition that other human beings are equally rational, intelligent, and competent to contribute to dialogues and discourses that we are part of. As such, considering the position of others is an act of faith in that it presents others an opportunity to question our ideas, and in the process, we have the opportunity to correct any errors and weaknesses in our thoughts and arguments.

Through listening, we open ourselves to the possibility of appreciating the differences we harbour with others who hold contrary views. If a misogynistic, racist, undemocratic, and sexist person is speaking, we have the moral, political, and ethical duty to listen to them, and use their arguments to strengthen ours. As such, we are in a position to go to war against their prejudices, against their facts and the way they present them, and in the process be in a position to stand in solidarity with our ideals, but at the same time, formulate our argument in ways that appeal to the people we listen to.

To listen, therefore, is an act of sincerity, a celebration of our faith in humanity, a triumph of our firm solidarity in ideals of democracy, equality, and social justice. It allows us to become students of society and participants in the pedagogy of listening. Listening offers participatory development practice, the methodological pathway, and the theoretical enlightenment that no other praxis does, thereby building the first foundation stone of development using a critical local resource, community spirit and strength. Critical pedagogy should offer student-participants the relevant tools and skills for digging deeper in their research so as to enrich their understanding of issues, places, and people. Alongside references to history should be content that exposes students to other cultures and ethnic diversities, thus challenging students to enter into unfamiliar epistemological territories. And this calls for a new pedagogy in the field, one in which teachers and students are co-learners. This is one way through which critical pedagogy can steer them towards a pedagogy that restores their faith in people – a pedagogy of seeing, a pedagogy of the future.

Questioning the dominant discourse

The pedagogy of *seeing* can also train students to listen and deliberately seek out alternative views. In response to the Brexit vote in the United Kingdom, Labour MP David Lammy (2016) would publish an opinion piece in the *Guardian* in which he called for a second referendum. Politicians and public intellectuals would repeat Lammy's language orthodoxy, with its paternalistic and condescending tone towards the people who voted for Brexit. There were demonstrations in the UK that seemed to blame the 'lies and untruths' that were 'promoted' by the Leave Campaign, which eventually motivated the ignorant and racist poor parts of the UK to vote to leave. This theme of ignorant and uneducated voters also appears in the American 'orthodoxy of language' in the aftermath of the infamous 2016 Trump victory. The mainstream media platforms seemed to fail to understand how a man seemingly careless with public statements which insulted many groups ended up winning the presidency.

For learners in critical pedagogy, it is vital that they unpack the underlying cultural and socio-political currents that motivate people to vote differently, even against their own interests. Scholar Lisa McKenzie (2016) offers a critical examination of the social and emotional context in which the majority of working-class communities and individuals voted for Brexit, and this applies to the post-Trump US as well. As if alluding to E.P. Thompson's (1963) praxis of history from below, McKenzie (2016) notes:

> *As a group of east London women told me: 'I'm sick of being called a racist because I worry about my own mum and my own child', and 'I don't begrudge anyone a roof who needs it but we can't manage either.' … Over the past 30 years there has been a sustained attack on working-class people, their identities, their work and their culture by Westminster politics and the media bubble around it. Consequently, they have stopped listening to politicians and to Westminster and they are doing what every politician fears: They are using their own experiences in judging what is working for and against them. … In the last few weeks of the campaign the rhetoric has ramped up and the blame game started. If we leave the EU it will be the fault of the 'stupid', 'ignorant', and 'racist' working class. Whenever working-class people have tried to talk about the effects of immigration on their lives, shouting 'backward' and 'racist' has become a middle-class pastime.*

What McKenzie is articulating here is an alternative discourse, one that sits in contrast to the discursive carnivalesque of *the view from here* as propagated by much of the neoliberal media establishment. What alternative perspectives do in the long term is to offer our students an opportunity to test the validity of the dominant discourse. After all, in *On Liberty,* John Stuart Mill (1859) cautions about the pitfalls of silencing 'that one person' or even humankind itself as it deprives an 'opportunity of exchanging error for truth', or 'the clearer perception and livelier impression of truth, produced by its collision with error'. There seems to have emerged a hegemony of defining, critiquing, and making sense of the world. In other cases, even the alternative perspectives have morphed into the dominant syntax. As such, critical pedagogy needs to go beyond the alternative perspectives and paradigms. This can be done through a pedagogy that challenges the dominance and colonization of alternative discourses that have transformed and mutated into dominant perspectives in which truth has become dehistoricized and fictionalized.

Thoughts for the future

It has been decades since Woodson released *Miseducation of the Negro*, Freire delivered *Pedagogy of the Oppressed*, and hook wrote *Teaching to Transgress*. The classroom – especially in development studies – continues to face serious questions about its relevance to the growing crisis that bedevils our society. The role of the development studies teacher, the curriculum, and the structure of the educational institution are also coming under increasing questions as to whether that education will liberate or continue to perpetuate years of oppression.

This chapter is not a strategy document on how to teach development. This is an ideological discussion about the transformative role of the teacher in producing transformative development field practitioners who can see with their heart. The aim is to connect the consciousness building efforts occurring in popular arts and movements to the need for similar efforts in the classroom. There is a need therefore to generate a kind of episte-mological frequency between the teacher and the student; between the content of the classroom and the reality and carnage out there; between the present and the future. There is a need to develop students who are highly critical of what they watch on television so that they do not end up constructing single stories of events and the world; there is a need to build the consciousness of students so that they understand the historical debates and struggles of women in our societies.

Teacher, teach me to see is a new manifesto of pedagogy, a pedagogy of being awake, a pedagogy for tomorrow. Being woke does not mean vindictiveness, a discourse of calling out people for ideological incorrectness or other concerns with marginalization. The teacher of critical pedagogy embodies significant roles beyond the mere transmitting of knowledge and information. For hooks, the teacher becomes more of a healer, a sage; one whose aim is not just to make lessons interesting or education critical. The teacher must accompany students on a journey of self-discovery, helping them to develop the relevant tools and skills that prepare them to be well-rounded individuals who understand and appreciate other ways of *seeing*, analysing, and sense-making.

The chapter therefore is about rescuing the teacher of critical pedagogy from becoming a status quo figure, one dislocated from social realities. This requires a new type of teacher who is not afraid to capture and explore critical issues with and alongside their students. A struggle for equality, social justice, democracy, and humanity is being waged the world over including in the classroom. It is the transformed classroom that must become a battle-ground for the development of minds of tomorrow, of empathetic, humane, and understanding beings with a resolve to make the world a great place for everyone.

Notes

1. I am grateful to Guy Bessette for these personal reflections on the manuscript.
2. Cadiz and Dagli outline the institutions involved in this learning network as comprising the College of Development Communication at the University of the Philippines, the Community-Based Natural Resource Management Learning Centre, the Centro Internacional de la Papa's Users' Perspectives with Agricultural Research and Development Asian network, the International Institute of Rural Reconstruction, and the Regional Community Forestry Training Centre for Asia and the Pacific.
3. Personal email from Cleofe Torres to Linje Manyozo on reviewing this manuscript, 5 December 2020.

CHAPTER 3
On empathy for the other

Mma Ramotswe felt that she needed to catch up on local news. There were always the newspapers, of course, but the real news, a complete picture of what was really happening, could only be gleaned from actual conversations with people. It was ordinary people who knew what was happening ... And the closer one got to the grassroots, the nearer one came to the people who actually experienced the effect of what was happening in the public world around them, the more complete one's understanding could become. (McCall Smith, 2012:209)

Building on the experiences of the afore-referenced protagonist, what this chapter seeks to do is to challenge teachers and educators of many examinations to build in our development students a sense of understanding other people by developing their engagement tools and skills. This is what empathy is all about. Mind Tools (2020) defines empathy as both the ability and the capacity to 'recognize emotions in others, to understand other people's perspectives on a situation, and use that insight to improve their mood and support them'.

Within the context of development pedagogy, what this does to a student of society is enable them to find others and engage with them, especially those who are different. This empowers them, in the words of Alexander McCall Smith above, to formulate a 'complete understanding' of the world, people, and phenomena. Likewise, Edward Said's revised introduction to *Orientalism* calls on humanity to study each other's cultures with compassion and understanding, so as to enrich our understanding of one another. One of the most enduring characteristics of the orthodox 'banking education', in Freirean sense, is its adherence to the prescribed curricula, which forces its participants and students to mechanistically think according to predetermined frameworks.

In this sense, the future deterministically becomes what Freire (1996b), in *Letters to Cristina*, elucidates as a 'given fact'. He describes this as the narrative characteristic of the orthodox education, in which the teacher is expected to teach what has been prescribed, and the student is expected to learn, swallow, and memorize all that the teacher provides – just like the mother bird regurgitates food to its chicks in the nest high up the tree.

This chapter therefore argues for a different kind of critical pedagogy: a *pedagogy of feeling*. Psychology tells us of the many forms of empathy – emotional, compassionate, and cognitive – all of which deal with people's feelings. This discussion recognizes that there are efforts in some institutions and processes of democracy to transform this banking education through more participatory and iterative approaches and practices. Yet, there is still this puritanical agglutination to what Freire conceived as the 'narrative character' of this banking education, largely because a fortuitous education intervention and programme is determined by its ability to have its graduates get jobs fast. Graduate employability and being job ready are some of the key performance indicators for most educational institutions of higher learning. What this chapter seeks thence is to release students from merely being depositories of teachers' knowledge and students of the prescribed curriculum. It's about students becoming more rounded participants who must learn to feel and *act*. I strongly believe cultivating in students the ability to feel, to feel for and feel with the other is one of the foundations of critical pedagogy.

What is empathy, really?[1]

Perhaps I could begin this conversation with a powerful observation by a group of wonderful women, led by the amazing Elizabeth Cady Stanton: 'The history of mankind is a history of repeated injuries [...] on the part of man toward woman, having in direct object the establishment of an absolute tyranny over her' (Stanton (1848/2015).

As pointed out, these are not my words – I have borrowed them from the *Declaration of Sentiments*, released by the organizers of the first ever women's rights convention held at Seneca Falls, New York in 1848. Now why should we begin a discussion of how Freire conceived empathy with an event that took place many years before Freire was even born, and before Freire (1996b) wrote *Pedagogy of the Oppressed* or *Letters to Cristina?* There are a number of issues, three to be specific, that I think are relevant to this discussion. Our conversation aims to highlight three main lessons that point to how Freire conceived empathy, alongside other attributes of love, humility, dialogue, and hope.

Freire's empathy

The Cambridge Dictionary (n.d.) definition of empathy seems to suggest that empathy is *the ability to understand and share the feelings of another person.* Yet, I think Freire goes deeper than that. For Freire, empathy is an action born of careful thoughtfulness in terms of its socio-political implications, in other words, a praxis. Such a praxis acknowledges our own shortfalls but is nevertheless informed by a growing socio-political consciousness of the factors that oppress an oppressed group. In Freirean terms, empathy is a form of *conscientização.*

Empathy as political solidarity

The first aspect of Freire's empathy that seems to come out of this particular event, the Seneca Falls Convention, is the notion of empathy as a form of political solidarity. Remember, Freire's work fluctuates between Marxism and

Christianity. The first aspect of empathy is empathy as a form of political solidarity, as a form of Marxist class struggle, in which a change agent or facilitator works with this oppressed group to produce this change. But before that can happen, there has to be a deeper conscientization, a deeper under-standing of the issues at play. Because Freire himself warns against fanaticism especially when one does not understand particular issues.

But here we are talking about empathy as a comprehensive form of consci-entization that allows us to acquire a decent understanding of the issues at play. Out of the 300 participants, the Declaration of Sentiments was signed by 100 people: 68 women and 32 men. At this time patriarchy was an official policy in and of this historic polity. To have 32 men openly contribute to the signing of this document was a concerted effort in acknowledging that society had a multitude of inequalities to confront and resolve in relation to women's issues. Hence the first aspect of Freire's conceptualization of empathy is this Marxist notion of empathy as a political praxis that allows one to identify with an oppressed group to transform the realities that oppress them.

Empathy as spiritual solidarity

The second aspect of Freire's empathy that is also critical comes from or has been articulated by the father of liberation theology, Father Gustavo Gutiérrez (1971), who introduces this notion of 'Preferential option for the Poor'. In many ways, the preferential option for the poor presupposes that while we may not be born into certain situations, we have the spiritual obligation to transform the realities of other people, because doing so is an expression of our absolute faith in God, this gratuitous love of God. Our ability to transform the realities of other people takes us back to the sermon on the mount in Matthew 5 where Jesus talks about the *Blessed* being the poor in spirit: '*Blessed* are those who mourn; *Blessed* are the meek; *Blessed* are those who hunger and thirst for righteousness.' Thence, we have this moral imperative to involve ourselves in the liberation of oppressed groups not necessarily because it will make us feel good, but because doing so expresses our love for God.

The very notion of preferential option for the poor seems to come out of this Declaration of Sentiments as well. Some of you who have read it might be wondering: What is Linje talking about? In actuality, the Declaration acknowledges God as the source of our equality. It is not in the consti-tution nor any document written by people, but it is God who endows us with the inalienable rights that make us equal – this is spelt clearly in the Declaration of Sentiments. I know that in much of the academy the very mention of God generates frowns ... it seems they dislike this idea of God or Jesus being cited. One of the things I admire about Freire is that he was very open in expressing his faith in God. He was transparent in acknowledging that whatever he did, in terms of the social struggles to liberate people, to contribute to the liberation of oppressed peoples was an expression of his faith in Jesus Christ. In fact, Freire talks about Marxism as a facility that enabled him to continue to express his love for Jesus Christ. There is no contradiction nor dichotomy.

Empathy as acknowledgement of the other

The third aspect of Freire's empathy that I think emerges from the *Declaration of Sentiments* is the acknowledgement of the other; to acknowledge the presence of the other. The very notion of the other places on us the political and moral duty to understand, appreciate, and acknowledge the presence of other people. The wonderful writer Roger Silverstone (1999), former head of media and communications at the London School of Economics and Political Science, writes in the book *Why Study the Media?* that in everything we do, whatever we write or whatever we say, the most important aspect is to understand other people – how we see other people, how we know them – to make sense of them. I believe empathy allows us to enter into the worlds of other people. It allows us to explore the worlds with which we are unfamiliar.

One criticism I have seen levelled considerably nowadays concerns problems of representing subalternity; that is, to put it cheaply, 'You are not black therefore you cannot understand the things affecting black people', or, 'You are not a woman therefore you cannot understand women or women's things', whatever that means. That is a very slippery and dangerous slope to trek: to assume that because someone was not born in a certain way, or because they were not born a certain race, they cannot understand certain issues. I believe all of us are born with an innate ability – the Creator endowed us with the ability to peer into other people's souls. So, it does not matter – if you are a woman you can still understand men, and even if you are not black, you can understand black people. Experience is important, yes – you can be born with a certain experience, but you can also learn from an experience. That experience can be cultural.

And that's why Edward Said (1978) writes in the revised Introduction to *Orientalism* (published after 11 September 2001 attacks in New York City) that we have the responsibility to study other people, not for the sake of exerting or validating our ignorance, but to enrich our understanding of other people and issues at play. That is what empathy does. It is a facility to conscientize us: to build our knowledge base around issues that may seem far-fetched or cultivated off-site.

Why then should we care about empathy, more especially today?

Our world today faces a myriad of challenges. There looms a dangerous climate crisis, environmental degradation, regional security threats as a result of increased and unnecessary militarization of powerful countries, ethnic tensions, ruthless class warfare ensuring that millions of men and women are left behind by capitalism and globalization, as well as serious cases of violence against women, girls, and children. The underlying issue in most of these challenges is a lack of understanding, lack of listening, and of course lack of empathy for the other.

This discussion highlights the power of empathy to improve the way we understand each other. In one of his last interviews before he passed away, Freire unpacked the praxis of empathy for us. He observed that 'it is through the exercise of tolerance that I discover the rich possibility of doing things and learning things with different people. Being tolerant is not a question of being naïve. On the contrary, it is a duty to be tolerant; an ethical duty, an historical duty, a political duty. But it does not demand from me that I lose my personality' (Freire, 1996a).

Like Freire, the Italian social theorist Antonio Gramsci (1932) believed in the collective power of men and women to make their own history. He writes in *The Prison Notebooks* that history seems to have 'deposited' within us an 'infinity of traces without leaving an inventory'. What empathy does, and this is how I think Freire articulates it, is allow us to work with other people, to contribute to the writing of a new inventory, to contribute to the construction and deconstruction of history, to the making and unmaking of history. After all, as pointed out by Edward Palmer Thompson (1963: 8), 'the working class did not rise like the sun at an appointed time', rather this oppressed group 'was present at its own making'. What this means, from the Gramscian and Freirean perspectives, is that the oppressed groups not only write their own history, but they name and interpret it as well, thus generating their own inventory.

The idea of feeling

There is an anathema that seems to have befallen many a teacher I have encountered: the curse of time. Time is on our mind as we start our lessons, making us wonder if we have enough material for the lectures, or if we have enough time to cover the material at hand – whether the students will be able to understand the material in the given time. One constant complaint or piece of feedback I and other teachers have received from students over the years is that there was not enough time to cover the material. Time becomes a factor in determining the quality and content of the curricula. Time, in other words, becomes an institutional spectre, more of an enemy or a liability than our friend.

As a result, the act of teaching has nowadays revolved around preparation and lesson plans, ensuring that the material is coherent enough to be covered in the given time. Teachers are spending an increased amount of time revisiting their slides, so much so that PowerPoint has become an institution in itself within that narrative education. Students are glued to the projector screen as the teacher's talking head goes through the material, and in cases where students have their own copies of the slides, they are busy adding notes and details to it. The relationship between the teacher and student, over and above being governed by time, is again being dictated and mediated by the material presence of the slides and the projector. There is no direct relationship between teachers and students as human beings.

In fact, this uncompromising adherence to the exemplum of the prescribed course and curriculum leaves little room to explore other issues that may not be central to the curriculum but are nevertheless critical in building the consciousness of the students and teachers as human beings. There is little or no room for *further human exploration*. I thus consider the structure of teaching and learning, its narrative character to be specific, to be a forest. The teaching institution, be it primary, secondary, tertiary or vocational, expects the teacher to lead and guide the students from one end of this proverbial forest to the other. The prescribed role of the teacher is to walk in front of the students showing them the safe paths, the places to cross the streams or to drink clean water as they all walk to the other side.

The chronicle attribute of orthodox education restricts the teacher to only showing the students this *given* path, which over moons, rivers, semesters, and academic years, becomes clearer and easier to walk as the teacher becomes more familiar with the direction itself. It explains why some teachers in tertiary institutions colonize certain subjects, teaching them over several years, thereby allowing themselves to be known as experts in such fields. This is not necessarily a bad idea as it sometimes empowers teachers to go beyond the *given script*. The danger however is that lessons become monotonous, the same master's voice year in, year out. There is no element of surprise, of *experimentation*. By the time the students come out the other side, they will be able, with the help of their notebooks which they used to take notes along the way, to explain the journey, the length, the challenges they faced, what they have learnt, and the like.

Prescribed outcomes

In fact, as the years go by and students from different intakes of the same course meet, they nostalgically reminisce about the good old days of walking through that proverbial forest of the classroom. They remind each other of the tricky paths, the sound of birds or animals, the thickness of the forest itself, the trepidation they faced on the journey, and, more critically, how that descriptive nature prepared them for the jobs they are doing. They report that the lessons were very practical. Education enables students to graduate into a ritual of mastering the dominant narrative and prescribed practice. A *habitude* of doing the same things creatively every year. Ritual has this performative temperament to appear creative, disruptive, and iterative – yet it has a stable and static customary foundation to it.

Over the course of the metaphoric forest journey, students who try to delve into the thick forests to whet their curiosity are scolded for 'going astray' and are warned of 'getting lost'. An increasing number of orthodox education (banking) teachers seem very much eager to claim that their teaching disrupts the descriptive character of education, yet feel threatened when genuinely disruptive students seek to explore the density of the forest on their own. Their knowledge, limited to the traditional role of escorting the students through this forest (which has transformed from an unknown to a known factor), feels threatened by the slightest suggestion that there are other ways of navigating the forest.

Education and learning are in the end reduced to the linear process of walking this given, prescribed, recommended, and well-known path that leads from point A of the forest to point B at the other side. The major advantage of this approach is that it allows teachers to complete their curriculum in the given time and also allows them to cover and engage with the curriculum satisfactorily. Knowledge becomes a commodity packaged within the variables of space and time and passed on to the expecting students. In fact, if time is a variable, the allocated time is even more critical.

There is little time to explore other variables. For example, symbolically speaking, the exploration of the forest is carried out during the day, such that it is inconceivable to think of exploring the forest at night. Night brings uncertainties. Night is unknown. Night is dangerous, unpredictable. Night disempowers the teacher because once their ability to *see* is hampered, they cannot comfortably traverse the forest, rendering them reliant on *other senses*: the collective input of the students. Their perception, largely trained to understand through seeing, cannot rely on new forms of navigation – of *feeling*, or of *listening*. Because the teacher's education was all about seeing and reliance on the power of seeing.

This symbolic act of seeing implies that all factors in teaching delivery are known elements. The authors, chapters, papers, books, arguments. These are critical elements to this *seeing*, the known factors. To think of exploring the forest at night may threaten the patterns of this sight whose depth of perception is hampered by the darkness, or even still, by leaving the road, and exploring the uncharted parts of the forest.

Let us consider a more practical example. 'When I do count the clock that tells the time', writes William Shakespeare in Sonnet 12, a magnificent poem that is both a lamentation and a hope. A lamentation of the ruthlessness of time: 'When I behold the violet past prime; The sable curls, all silvered over with white.' Here, time is this belligerent enemy that takes away the youth, beauty, virility, and mobility of plants and humans. Yet there is also hope with a capital H that even if time is this enemy who will take us to the graveyard, we can still cheat death: 'And nothing 'gainst Time's scythe can make defence; Save breed, to brave him when he takes thee hence.' That by having children, we can escape death.

Teaching this poem would require a teacher *to see* the critical variables. The grammar of Shakespeare, the structure of his poems, the *Soneto* (with a specific number of lines, 14, a specific rhyme schema and structured in three quatrain and a couplet). This is the *line of sight* for the teacher. The figurative day. The *known and given* road from one end of the forest to the other.

But Shakespeare's forest is also an unknown terrain. And the question is: can a teacher really teach Shakespeare without paying attention to these unknowns? Are these unknowns even relevant? It is well known to history that Shakespeare was 18 when he married his wife, Anne Hathaway, who was 26 at the time (Honan, 1998). The gap of eight years is significant. Could it be possible Anne would symbolically be both an older sister and a mother to the teenage Shakespeare? Why should we even read beyond the lines and not 'just stick to the poems'? Well, the poems were about love and relationships to women. In fact, another unknown that seems to be relevant in this discussion is that when he died in 1616 at age 52, Shakespeare had just signed his will, which left much of his estate to the eldest child, Susanna, with specific instructions that she should pass it on to her first son (Honan, 1998). Perhaps his attitude towards women could also be explored in the fact that his will rarely mentions his wife, though he did leave to her one of their beds (Honan, 1998).

These are seemingly irrelevant facts to the study of the romance and structure of the *sonnets*. Yet the critical factor is that in today's world, there is an increasing level of violence against women and children. Even if we are not accusing Shakespeare of this particular vice, students of society should ask the relevant questions: Why specify that his wealth should go to his grandson? Why leave but a bed to a woman who had cared for him from his teenage years? Having lost his son in infancy, could it be that he regretted not having a son? Does society give prominence and value to having boys over girls? Is it possible to be romantic towards women and simultaneously carry in us patriarchal views towards these same women? The discussion of the content of the poems should thus be mediated by the historical context in which these poems were written, because that allows for the students to *feel the material conditions* in which they live. This is what the British writer Raymond Williams conceived as the *structure of feeling*.

Exploring the unknown

Coming back to the symbolic forest, we know it is alive with secrets. There exists an entire self-balanced ecosystem. Once we leave the prescribed path, we are faced with the challenge of exploring the unknown, unseen, unfelt – the dangerous. As aptly captured by Ngũgĩ wa Thiong'o (1977) in *Petals of Blood*, students and their teacher will see worms eating plants and yet the plants do not eat back. They will see flowers blooming on which bees extract nectar for their own honey production, pollinating the plants in the process and allowing them to reproduce. Wouldn't it be equally critical to discuss with the students how this *order of things* is a microcosm of real life in and out of the forest? Wouldn't it be the right time to explore what empirical examples of those same situations exist in front of them? Do violence and inequality have their own structure?

Attempting to answer these questions with students is critical pedagogy in practice, as it allows both the teacher and students to move from the praxis of seeing to the praxis of feeling. What does it feel like to be a woman, married to a man for so many years who then left little or nothing to her? What if it were my sister or daughter that Shakespeare did this to? How does it feel to read his romantic poems knowing this small but critical fact? This praxis of feeling is very much uncharted territory for this narrative education. It therefore requires that the teacher and students raise fundamental questions about their own attitude and views towards women and the world in general.

The *praxis of feeling* becomes a necessary facility for exploring this forest besides *seeing*. By feeling the learning material, knowledge begins to become relevant to the daily and lived realities of the participants in the educational process. Feeling then becomes a platform for imagining the emotions of the 'other', which is what empathy is all about. Empathy allows us to imagine, see, and feel what the other person, the person who is different is feeling right now. Writing to journalist Hamilton Nolan (2014) of *Gawker Media* before his 2014 execution by the State of Texas, then death row inmate Ray Jasper explored this fundamental question of empathy, as a form of feeling:

> I think 'empathy' is one of the most powerful words in this world that is expressed in all cultures ... I do not own a dictionary, so I can't give you the Oxford or Webster definition of the word, but in my own words, empathy means 'putting the shoe on the other foot.' ... Empathy. A rich man would look at a poor man, not with sympathy, feeling sorrow for the unfortunate poverty, but also not with contempt, feeling disdain for the man's impoverished state, but with empathy, which means the rich man would put himself in the poor man's shoes, feel what the poor man is feeling, and understand what it is to be a poor man. Empathy breeds proper judgement. Sympathy breeds sorrow. Contempt breeds arrogance. Neither are proper judgements because they're based on emotions. That's why two people can look at the same situation and have totally different views. We all feel differently about a lot of things. Empathy gives you an inside view. It doesn't say 'If that was me ...', empathy says, 'That is me.'

In the aforementioned, Jasper discusses empathy as providing this 'inside view' that enables a person to formulate 'proper judgement'. This is the determination about what could be the right question, about things, about people, about places, and about the world. This differs from sympathy, or what John Stuart Mill in *Essays on Liberty* conceives as 'fellow feeling'.

Reading the world

A major contribution from liberatory theology and education is the development of an emotional consciousness and percipience that allows students to, in Freire's terms, not just read the word, but read the world too.

Reading the world implies that we become students of society, students of the human condition. Instead of listening to master narratives about people and places, we employ our sharp perceptiveness to investigate things for ourselves without relying on other people's prejudices or judgements. This is an important attribute that students should have.

When I first moved to Australia in 2004 to read for a PhD, I developed a tendency to travel and visit rural and regional areas, largely because I grew up in rural communities in Africa. Even as I returned some years ago to take up a teaching post, I was always passionate about visiting and exploring these regional areas, largely because I found an emotional connection to these places. I was warned, however – sharply warned by mostly white friends and colleagues – to be careful of 'these rural and regional people', that they have the tendency to be racist, narrow-minded, and parochial. Yet as I continued visiting these regions and places, I would find out how hospitable most of these 'narrow-minded' people were; they warmly received me, sometimes inviting me into their homes.

It would be naïve to think and assume there is no racism or discrimination, but the point is that as I have increased my interaction with rural and regional communities, I have become empathetic to their situation; I have become much more understanding. They have been marginalized by years of centralized policy making in Canberra, Sydney or Melbourne; they have almost been forgotten in policies and plans. Places like Yinnar and Boolara are not even on the national gas grid. Worse, the main coal power plants that used to provide jobs and economic security to these regional communities have closed or are just closing down. With loss of jobs and opportunities come many social evils: emigration of young and skilled workers, drugs and alcohol abuse, mental health, crime, and so forth.

As with most regional communities in Africa, these regional Australian communities have tended in some cases to be inward-looking, to rely on themselves and not wait on government promises. The more I have increased my interactions, the more I have appreciated, understood, and respected their resilience. I would eventually move to one of these regional towns myself. Empathy challenges us to put the shoe on what Jasper says is the 'other foot'. This process of putting the shoe on the other foot is an active process, not just a one-day public relations exercise, where politicians sit with communities in the sand to listen to local perspectives. It is about *reading the world* we live in.

Such a process challenges students and their teachers to go beyond the prescribed content and methods of knowledge dissemination and exchange. They should begin to question the stereotypes and assumptions surrounding critical issues in society and how they affect marginalized groups such as women, children, people with disability or ethnic minorities. This approach is very much like abandoning the known and usual path in our proverbial forest.

In a class on developing social and behaviour change communications, I did, at one point, discuss the use of the traditional P-Process (Health

Communication Capacity Collaborative, 2013) with my students, and how critical it is for communication managers to be strategic about these interventions. There are two ways to embark on this proverbial unknown in the forest. First, when teaching students about development theory and practice, the tendency is to give examples from the global South. Yet I shared with the students a *BBC News Online* article that discussed the rise of syphilis and gonorrhoea in Australia, especially among indigenous populations (Mao, 2018). I did this for several reasons.

The first was to show development challenges still bedevil the global North, where homelessness, early marriages, child poverty, domestic violence, and increasing socio-economic inequality are on the increase. As such, development communication approaches are very much relevant to the global North. The second reason was to show the correlation between economic marginalization and inequality on one hand and the spread of diseases on the other. The third was to stimulate debate about the marginalization of Indigenous Australians.

It is thus almost impossible to imagine developing relevant health communication strategies and plans that would address the key information and communication needs of the targeted populations without having the students think about issues of social and economic inequality. Why are indigenous populations being affected by these STIs? Why rural and regional populations? How do we reach out to these populations? Once we begin to think of indigenous and rural populations as target audiences of our communication campaigns, we are equally compelled to think of them as human beings: What are their lives like? What does it mean to live in rural and regional areas? How many kids go to school in these areas? What are the rates of early pregnancies? What about family violence? Do people have access to doctors and proper medical services? A can of worms is opened. Eventually, students embark on a journey into Joseph Conrad's emblematic 'heart of darkness', the deepest sojourn into the interior of the allegorical forest – indigenous colonization and marginalization.

Through exploring these unknowns, our students begin to understand that such rising rates of STIs are not just about the lack of proper information: that there are larger and more complex structural issues at play. The political economy of society is a key determinant in the way people behave and respond to social issues. The students then realize the connection between demand and supply; that telling people about condoms (demand creation) is one thing, but having condoms available (the supply) is another. And even if they are available, do the people want to use them?Are they motivated enough to use them? If they are not motivated to do so, what is going on in their lives to make them not care about the risks of unprotected sex?

Exploring these issues will lead students to empathize, or what Jasper describes as the act of 'putting the shoe on the other foot': What does it mean to be a resident living in indigenous and rural areas? What is it like being an Indigenous person? It is the exploration of this uncharted territory by the teacher and students that allows for a critical rethink of how policies in indigenous communities are driven by political and not necessarily social or local interests.

The consequence of this realization is that it allows for the generation of Jasper's 'proper judgement'. In the case of students of society, instead of being restricted to the prescribed curriculum of developing health communications to address the rise in the rates of STIs, their exposure to and empathy with indigenous issues and people will enable them to become better policy makers, especially when it comes to dealing with people that are different and have been left behind.

Psychology Today Australia (n.d.) defines empathy as an experience of understanding another person's thoughts, feelings, and condition from their point of view, rather than from one's own. As such, empathy is not just this act of 'putting the shoe on the other foot', but more critically, it is an 'experience of understanding', which is born out of careful and considerate learning of a situation at hand. The experience may have been lived or acquired through mediatization.

What is significant in our study of health communication is that bringing in a case study that affects both indigenous and non-indigenous communities offers a platform for raising questions about established patterns of socio-economic marginalization and inequality. It thus offers a platform for developing this 'experience in understanding' of the social determinants of health among indigenous populations. In our symbolic forest, the purpose might be to learn how to develop social and behaviour change communications strategically, using the prescribed models preferred by governments, educational institutions, and research entities. Yet the teacher has allowed what bell hooks considers the 'transgression' of the official curriculum by encouraging students to explore the depths of the forest, in this case indigenous inequality.

Am I empathetic?

As development practitioners we often assume that we are empathetic, since we tend to surround ourselves with those we work with – and work with very well. As a result, we tend not to pay critical attention to how we engage with others. Meanwhile numerous scholarly studies and workplace guidelines use ambiguous and general terms to suggest how we can display empathy: some suggestions include trying new things, requesting feedback, avoiding biases, treating people nicely, and listening to people. But isn't this what we think we are doing most of the time anyway? The popular American talk show host Ellen DeGeneres, who has been known to promote kindness in people, faced scrutiny after numerous staff and hosts of her show reported bullying and cold-heartedness from the host and a number of senior staff. So, the question is, what safeguards can we put in place to ensure we are empaths? Table 1 presents some proposals based on the three types of empathy outlined by MindTools (2020).

Table 1 Empathy in Development Practice

Empathy	Explanation	Soul-searching questions	Practical actions in development practice
Emotional empathy	Sharing another's feelings, such as when in love	How do they feel about this? How different are our feelings about this? Where should I adjust in order to meet them in between?	Spend time listening to people without a notebook Recall what they said and then take notes long after the meeting Speak with humility
Cognitive empathy	Comprehension of another's thoughts and feelings	What are they thinking? What is their point of view? What do they feel about an issue at hand?	Begin the next meeting by summarizing what they told you without referring to the notes Be able to articulate their argument while asking them for validation Ask people about their life experiences Make sure you remember these in the next encounters Sit with the people, and reject positions of authority
Compassionate empathy	Both understanding of and active engagement to resolve another's emotions	What practical efforts have they put in place to try to resolve this? Why has it not worked out? Where and how can I help?	Dress like a local Memorize and remember people's names in meetings Join local people in daily activities Learn the local songs and performances Participate in innovations

Thoughts for the future

This chapter has explored interesting options that would ideally enable and empower teachers within traditional classrooms and who are restricted by the dictates of prescribed curricula to create liminal spaces in which they can provide education that builds empathy in students. Increasing populations and limited places in schools, colleges, and universities mean that institutions have converted into knowledge mills, in which learning has been stripped of its functional attribute as a constructive facility for exploring significant epistemological questions that confront our society today. Education has become commoditized, with a focus on business models that bring in new students while getting rid of the old.

The space for the teacher to experiment with genuine questions of learning is disappearing; this space where they have the time and opportunity to challenge students to think deeply about engaging with the fundamental questions facing our world today. As employers demand *job ready* students, educational institutions are forced to look at *graduate employability* indices as a guiding principle. After all, there is serious competition for high university rankings, research grants, and increased focus on managing institutions as businesses – thus there is this intense corporatization of education. The result is that the guiding compass for teaching and learning are certain arbitrary indicators that have little to do with developing the totality of the human experience of the student. Nothing else.

To talk about developing values raises questions, because it is not considered an output – students can learn these values at home, at church, and other social institutions within society. The teacher is expected to focus on providing education, the coverage and completion of that symbolic path from point A through the forest to point B. Values are immaterial. What it means is that we are training generations of young professionals with adequate technical knowledge, but without a developed sense of key human values. These are significant values which transcend ideological diversity – values like empathy, love, and forgiveness. What we have are young professionals who often lack emotional intelligence, and this lack can perhaps be extended to the broader social sphere, particularly when we consider the often-derisive debates on major issues which trigger knee-jerk reactions rather than a deeper level of understanding. Preparing students to develop a value sensitive approach can aid society.[2]

This chapter has argued for a more radical and proactive teaching pedagogy; one that creates intellectual space in the curriculum and classroom to cover both the prescribed and *experimental* text. The experimental text is *hidden*, lying within the prescribed text, and offers teachers and students the time and space to build human values as they acquire knowledge. And in cases where the teacher has more leverage over the content of their curriculum, they would be able to play around with more experimental texts while challenging students to develop the important virtue of empathy.

In a society being torn apart by the deafening sounds of speaking at the same time, where social media is encouraging us to speak more (be it Twitter, Instagram or Facebook), citizens are taking up these opportunities; in some cases, these platforms are amplifying voices of marginalized groups who would have otherwise been forgotten and footnoted from history. Yet amid all this speaking lies a need to listen to each other, to build more understanding, to build more bridges in the way we think about the future of our communities.

Empathy is a significant human value which, by its very nature, empowers and prepares citizens to take a back seat and build understanding with people they may have serious disagreements with. Empathy is not necessarily naïveté – it is an exercise in tolerance. As a human value, it offers, at best, all of us an opportunity to listen to one another, to reach across our differences, to lower our voices and respectfully communicate our arguments even if we are hanging on to the last threads of our patience and temperament.

The *pedagogy of seeing and feeling* is a praxis that allows both student and teacher to take a deep breath, then 'breathe'. To 'breathe' implies letting go of all the anger, suspicions, and stereotypes, and accepting for once that across from ourselves, right in front, stands another human being who suffers like us. And then we look at the world from their perspective; in Jasper's language, we 'put the shoe on the other foot'. Teaching students to see another's perspective should be a fundamental responsibility of the transformative teacher. It is a political duty. So that, as advised by Mma Ramotswe in the opening of this chapter, students of society are able to formulate a 'complete understanding' of the world, which helps us to make proper judgements.

Notes

1. This section was first shared as a presentation, 'On empathy for the other', as part of the Paulo Freire Centennial Celebrations in preparation for the next 100 years. Organized by the Institute for Media and Creative Industries at Loughborough University, 17 March 2021. https://www.paulofreirecentennial.org/principal-in/
2. Appreciation to Julia Bernardo for such illuminating conversations.

CHAPTER 4
On women in development

It must be constantly borne in mind that the committed Algerian woman learns both her role as "a woman alone in the street" and her revolutionary mission instinctively … The Algerian woman is not a secret agent. It is without apprenticeship, without briefing, without fuss, that she goes out into the street with three grenades in her handbag or the activity report of an area in her bodice … She does not have the sensation of playing a role she read about ever so many times in novels or seen in motion pictures … What we have here is not the bringing to light of a character known and frequented a thousand times in imagination or in stories. It is an authentic birth in a pure state, without preliminary instruction. There is no character to imitate. On the contrary, there is an intense dramatization, a continuity between the woman and the revolutionary. The Algerian woman rises directly to the level of tragedy (Fanon, 1965:50).

This chapter interrogates the question of women in development by examining the notion of 'feminism from below' or what can be conceived as *organic feminism*, tracing it to four sources. First is Frantz Fanon, who, in the quote above, conceives it as the subaltern woman's 'authentic birth in pure state, without pure instruction'. Usually lying on the periphery or outside both modernity and globalization, but shaped by both as well as local traditions and, in some cases, indigenous knowledge, feminism in its organic state is being conceptualized as unwritten rules, regulations, and experiences that enlist oppressed women in social struggles at birth. Such enlisting of oppressed women happens 'without preliminary instruction', ensuring that there is 'continuity between the woman and the revolutionary' (Fanon, 1965: 50). In this case feminist struggle is not a choice that a subaltern woman has to make; rather, her only option is to rise 'directly to the level of tragedy'; that is, engage in life-long struggles for her liberation.

Second is E.P. Thompson's notion of history from below, in which he discusses how the working class, the unemployed, the underclass, and peasantry actively participate in writing their own history. Thompson (1963) conceives the distinction between what is history proper, and the history of and written by oppressed groups. Writing in this case does not necessarily entail western literacy, rather it involves and celebrates performed resistance, in which the daily lives of oppressed groups and their forms of expression (such as music, dressing style, use of the body, and so forth) become artefacts of resistance.

Third is the notion of organic as it figures in organic feminism, which emerges from social theory – starting with Gramsci's notions of organic intellectuals. Intellectuals as a concept comes from Marx, believing that powerful classes that control production eventually control mental production and ideological facilities. Years later, a keen student of Marx (1852/2010), Antonio Gramsci (1932), would, in *The Prison Notebooks*, contend that control over material production provides the impetus for oppressive classes to exercise control over 'mental production', in other words, capitalist monopoly is a priori for knowledge monopoly.

Fourth, is the notion of subaltern speech as articulated by Gayatri Spivak (1988). Spivak mases a strong case for appreciating the use of both the body of the woman as a script in their social struggles – even if it means employing strategies and tactics that could result in the loss of lives. Borrowing from Fanon, Thompson, Gramsci, and Spivak, therefore, one could argue that organic feminist struggles entail communicative practices created and naturalized by oppressed women themselves in an attempt to write their own history – not necessarily to counter narratives of patriarchy, modernity, and capitalism, but out of the need for authentic self-expression and liberation.

Women as intellectuals of their struggle

Granted, the concept of intellectuals emerges from Marx and Hegel's discussions in *A Critique of German Ideology*, central to which is this idea that social change is made possible by the ideological leadership which is developed and supported by common men and women. For this chapter, the idea is that feminism is made and curated by women in all their diversity. For this to happen, there is a need for a revolutionary group to form its own intellectuals to help the oppressed group theorize and explain its struggle. In fact, the first ever Women's Congress in 1848 held in New York, emphasized the need to celebrate the equality of men and women. The *Declaration of Sentiments*, agreed to by the Congress attendees, does recognize how patriarchy has oppressed women – and how feminism becomes a necessary reaction to free women from such oppressive superstructure: 'He has compelled her to submit to laws, in the formation of which she had no voice.' Or, 'He has endeavoured, in every way that he could, to destroy her confidence in her own powers, to lessen her self-respect, and to make her willing to lead a dependent and abject life' (Stanton, 1848/2015).

In this case, feminism becomes that exogenous intervention, very reactionary, and in any case, affiliated with modernity and progressive politics. And Fanon criticizes this exogenous model of feminism, that is usually created within the space of civil society politics, by movements and organizations that are created to contest state power. Exogenous feminism is a result of this contestation of power over various aspects that shape women's public life. For example, Fanon examines the contestation of the traditional veil worn by the Algerian women, which became 'the bone of contention in a grandiose battle, on account of which the occupation forces ... were to mobilise their most powerful and most varied resources, and in the course of which the colonised were to display a surprising force of inertia' (Fanon, 1965: 36, 37). In this case, exogenous feminism is about invading women's spaces:

> *The indigent and famished women were the first to be besieged. Every kilo of semolina distributed was accompanied by a dose of indignation against the veil and the cloister. The indignation was followed up by practical advice. Algerian women were invited to play 'a functional, capital role' in the transformation of their lot. They were pressed to say no to a centuries-old subjection. The immense role they were called upon to play was described to them. The colonial administration invested great sums in this combat* (Fanon, 1965: 38).

In this contestation, there emerges the role of the NGOs and civil society in perpetuating this colonial agenda: 'Mutual aid societies and societies to promote solidarity with Algerian women sprang up in great numbers' (ibid.). And as such feminism became an instrument of western modernity: 'We want to make the Algerian ashamed of the fate that he metes out to women' (ibid.). Feminism became both an instrument and political doctrine for undermining the traditional society Lerner conceived as being a stumbling block to achieving modernity and economic development: 'If we want to destroy the structure of Algerian society, its capacity for resistance, we must first of all conquer the women; we must go and find them behind the veil where they hide themselves and, in the houses, where the men keep them out of sight' (ibid.: 37, 38).

So how does exogenous feminism work? It does not matter whether it has western origins or southern origins, exogenous feminism assumes that women's struggles, especially for southern women, lie outside their bodies. That it is the role of external players to sensitize them to their rights and responsibilities. Well, Gayatri Spivak's seminal piece, 'Can the subaltern speak', debunks that myth. Spivak, like Fanon, acknowledges that any oppressed woman, such as Bhuvaneswari in 1920s India, usually curates spaces to contest colonialism, capitalism, and patriarchy. Thence, an oppressed woman cannot be taught feminism, because she is feminism. Yet for exogenous feminism, the civilizing role of the woman in helping deconstruct the traditional society especially by non-state actors seems critical:

> *In the colonialist program, it was the woman who was given the historic mission of shaking up the Algerian man. Convening the woman, winning her over to the foreign values, wrenching her free from her status, was at the same time achieving a real power over the man and attaining a practical, effective means of destructuring Algerian culture ... Unveiling this woman is revealing her beauty; it is baring her secret, breaking her*

> *resistance, making her available for adventure ... There is in it the will*
> *to bring this woman within his reach, to make her a possible object of*
> *possession* (Fanon, 1965: 39, 43–44).

Building on this notion of organic feminism, how do we begin to think of women in development, especially women from the global South? Are oppressed women from the global South the same as their counterparts in the north? How does one analyse the question of women in development then? Perhaps we could start with the key attributes of this organic feminism, or feminism from below.

First is that the woman in organic feminism is invisible. Not because they are not there, but they have this tendency not to be seen. The degree of invisibility might differ between oppressed women from the south and their counterparts in the north. The oppressed woman from the south is usually materially invisible. She rarely owns property, or appears registered in most official documents; her presence is footnoted, and in numerous cases, she becomes a little more visible when supported by or seen alongside male identity. Worse, is that because of the weak state, the fate and welfare of this southern woman is left to the power of traditional governance institutions and non-state actors. Yes, the oppressed woman in the north is also invisible, but at least they have some level of access to state and non-state resources – offering them at least some access to social mobility. Nevertheless, what does this oppressed woman look like?

In the battle for Algeria's independence from colonial France, Fanon conceived this oppressed female as 'This woman who sees without being seen frustrates the coloniser; There is no reciprocity. She does not yield herself, does not give herself, does not offer herself; The Algerian has an attitude toward the Algerian woman – which is on the whole clear. He does not see her' (Fanon, 1965: 44). On the part of the colonized woman, alongside this invisibility is the trait to co-exist with oppression: 'Holding out against the occupier on this precise element means inflicting upon him a spectacular setback; it means more particularly maintaining "co-existence" as a form of conflict and latent warfare. It means keeping up the atmosphere of an armed truce' (ibid.: 47) This co-existence entails undergoing 'important modifications; These innovations are of particular interest since they were at no time included in the programme of the struggle. The doctrine of the Revolution, the strategy of combat, never postulated the necessity for a revision of forms of behaviour with respect to the veil' (ibid.).

The second attribute entails the ability to adapt to new forms of struggle, granted that the anti-revolutionary forces have been able to adapt their oppressive strategies to changing times and situations. In this case therefore, Fanon (1965: 48) argues:

> *the decision to involve women as active elements of the Algerian*
> *Revolution was not reached lightly. In a sense, it was the very conception*
> *of the combat that had to be modified. The violence of the occupier,*

his ferocity, his delirious attachment to the national territory, induced
the leaders no longer to exclude certain forms of combat; The women's
entry into the war had to be harmonised with respect for the revolu-
tionary nature of the war.

The third attribute concerns the ability of the woman to carry out revolutionary tasks based on her prescribed traditional roles. As observed by
Fanon (1965: 53), the women would carry messages, 'of complicated verbal
orders learned by heart, sometimes despite complete absence of schooling',
and sometimes they would stand guard or watch, conduct spying missions,
nurse the injured, carry dangerous weapons through tight roadblocks,
carry dangerous weapons and even commit acts of extreme violence.
The women who became 'wholly and deliberately immersed in the revolutionary action' did this even at the risk to their own safety knowing the
violence of the colonizer (ibid.: 57). Because there is a link between her
revolutionary and traditional roles, 'the unveiled Algerian woman moves
like a fish in the Western waters' (ibid.: 58). After all, for Fanon (1965:
59–61, 63):

The shoulders of the unveiled Algerian woman are thrust back with
easy freedom. She walks with a graceful, measured stride, neither too
fast nor too slow. Her legs are bare, not confined by the veil, given
back to themselves, and her hips are free ... The veil covers the body
and disciplines it, tempers it, at the very time when it experiences its
phase of greatest effervescence. The veil protects, reassures, isolates ...
The Algerian woman is not only in conflict with her body. She is a
link, sometimes an essential one, in the revolutionary machine ...
Removed and resumed again and again, the veil has been manipulated,
transformed into a technique of camouflage, into a means of struggle.
The virtually taboo character assumed by the veil in the colonial
situation disappeared almost entirely in the course of the liberating
struggle ... The veil helped the Algerian woman to meet the new
problems created by the struggle.

The quote emphasizes the fluidity with which southern women combine
traditional and revolutionary roles. In doing so, these revolutionary women
ensure that the 'flower of the word will not die' and that 'the word which
came from the depth of history and the earth can no longer be cut by
the arrogance of the powerful' (Zapatista Movement, 1996). Often, these
feminist struggles from below are not about development or progress,
women just want to survive or, in the words of my grandmother, 'just to
breathe'. The literal Chichewa word she used is, *kupuma. Kupuma* means a
number of things. Literally it means to breathe in and out. Just breathing.
But then *kupuma* also means to rest (after working hard). Feminism in the
global South entails that – the struggle to breathe – without which all other
human endeavours are impossible.

In fact, in *Pluriverse*, Kothari et al. (2019) note that much of the global South is focusing on survival and not progress or development. In this case, therefore, it is not easy to find many encounter points where the survival needs of southern women coincide with progressive needs of upper class, working, and bourgeois women. An interesting debate in the US concerns Roe v Wade – which has just been overturned. While a woman's right to choose should be their choice, it shouldn't be lost on us that Margaret Sanger (the founder of Planned Parenthood) did propose a Negro Project, with the aim of reducing the black population.[1] As such, some western feminist struggles are antagonistic towards southern women's interests.

The empirical context

The experience of women is of paramount significance in the times we live in – a period marked by increased cases of violence against women and girls, socio-economic exclusion, plus the #MeToo and other transformative rights-based movements advocating for the increased visibility and inclusion of women. The following chapter challenges development thinkers and practitioners on how best to engage with the prospect of quintessential equality being released in the age of religious and cultural diversity. This is an era when women have become a critical subject of sustainable development goals, but also an epoch where societies are being challenged to broaden their views, definitions, and treatment of women. In that endeavour, the role of the educator of critical pedagogy becomes paramount in motivating their students to engage with the inclusion, diversity, and equity in this evolving discourse by and about women. This chapter expects development practitioners to familiarize themselves with feminist thinking and practices in order to better handle these issues in deliberative development.

It must be pointed out, however, that this is a very formidable chapter to write, not least because I am a man, but because I am writing at a time when questions of voice and authority in representation are continuously being contested. It has reached a point where some academics and activists postulate a man has no right writing about women's issues. Bonny Cassidy highlights that 'it is worth adding here, that even the idea of "women's issues" as an exclusive concern or special interest might be contested', after all, both 'critical masculinity and #MeToo have called for women's rights to become everybody's business'.[2] This brings me to the two questions that have necessitated the writing of this chapter.

The first conundrum concerns the debate on the *prerogative to represent others*. The question is, who should represent 'others' or, in this case, who should represent women? These debates have been explored by scholars over the years. In the early 1900s, Robert Flaherty (1922) would travel to the Canadian Arctic to document the lives of the indigenous Inuit. Gayatri Spivak's (1988) 'Can the subaltern speak?' provided a postcolonial critique of how voices by oppressed women are depoliticized and misunderstood by privileged classes. To an extent, anthropologist Johannes Fabian (1990) recognizes the different layers of challenges with representing the other. Even if evidence suggests that both men and women can represent women, to avoid a women-only echo chamber, the question remains, *who should represent women in development interactions?*

The second question asks, *what kind of feminist thinking should shape development interactions?* It deconstructs western feminism as propounded in classic philosophy, such as that of John Stuart Mill (1859; 1859/2017). In *The Subjection of Women*, Mill (1859/2017: 1) raises concerns with 'moralities of submission', arguing to have them replaced with 'a principle of perfect equality'. Various forms of non-western feminism have offered alternative perspectives and practices of equality; therefore, it is possible for women who are traditional and religious to be considered feminist. As southern feminist scholar Saba Mahmood (2005) and others demonstrate, there is no homogeneous feminism nor homogeneous women.

This chapter considers the dilemma of discussing the subject of women in both development classrooms and practice. I am not just referring to teaching feminism to development practitioners; rather, granted feminism is a political and theoretical *praxis* for consolidating women's visibility in the polity, it should be emphasized that we can discuss women without feminism. After all, even feminism itself is ideological and not homogeneous. Yet for this discussion, I wish to highlight the significance of discussing women and women's experiences in relation to feminism and why it is important in a broader sense, without getting into the various aggradations of modern feminist theory and practice. Feminism is, after all, a 'shifting landscape and a work in progress'. What is paramount is that we are capacitating development practitioners of the field to broaden their views on women and on gendered structures; to understand that they need to be able to engage with feminism and even embrace it to lead to greater inclusion. Men need to be taught to engage with these discourses, to see themselves as a part of modern universalist feminism.

As pointed out by Spivak, Mahmood, Djebar, Mohanty, and other postcolonial feminists, feminism in the west has different agendas from those of the many forms of southern feminism. In fact, before feminism itself, there were radical practices and philosophies that emphasized both the equality and excellence of women in various facets of life. And outside modern and southern feminism are traditional and religious practices and movements that are gradually transforming oppressive hegemonies – one meeting, song or newsletter at a time. As bell hooks (1991) confesses, feminist practice is grounded in heterogeneous human experiences. This study covers four crucial areas that teachers of critical pedagogy can pay attention to through assignments, class discussions, and general reflections. These areas are not exhaustive, but nevertheless comprise representations of women, colonial feminism, and the celebration of women's role in development.

The challenge of representing women

One challenge facing the praxis of representation of the 'other' concerns generating portrayals that speak to the needs and realities of living people. The American anthropologist Jay Ruby (1991) observes that when it comes to producing or making sense of such representations, our attention should focus on 'questions of voice, authority, and authorship'. Johannes Fabian (1990) seems to suggest that representations of the other experience fractured power relations, and often end up as re-enactment or performances. Ruby then proposes a form of cooperative representation that brings subjects into the process of negotiating how they want to be seen. Focusing specifically on the filmic genre, Ruby (1991: 50) observes that such cooperative representations offer 'the possibility of perceiving the world from the viewpoint of the people who lead lives that are different from those traditionally in control of the means for imaging the world'. Such multiple perspectives also speak to the fact that even the experiences of women will always vary greatly.

As such, when representing others, an important starting point is *perspective*. Negotiated representations allow us to see the world from the viewpoint of those who experience history – in this case, women. Global debate arose when Angelina Jolie directed the 2011 film *In the Land of Blood and Honey*, which told the story of Bosnian Muslim women who were raped during the Serbian conflict. The question then was, and has always been, can a white, privileged woman tell the story of 'other women' who are oppressed? Can she tell the story of Muslim women who were raped? Can she offer a decent account on anything other than white privilege? Which brings us to the questions for this discussion: How do we discuss representations of women in the classroom? And how do we discuss women in such a way that empowers young men to appreciate the struggles women endure?

One challenge of making assumptions about women – especially image makers such as Jolie – is that identities are not singular, but a collection of experiences that shape us over time. Jolie is much more than just a white woman. Her compassion for other women and their suffering is well documented in her activism. To suggest that she has no moral authority to produce or direct such a movie because of her skin colour is then restricting her to defining herself as a white woman.

In the Land of Blood and Honey offers us an opportunity to learn more about the experiences of women during war. In a similar vein, *Their Eyes Were Watching God* is a novel written by a black woman, Zora Neale Hurston (1937). It tells the story of Janie Crawford, a curious teen who matures into adulthood, abandons her marriage, then runs away with a younger lover as part of a journey of self-discovery. This is, among many, one film that teachers and students of critical pedagogy ought to watch and discuss. It may be an American story from the 1920s and 30s, but it speaks to what many subaltern women such as my mother are all about. A woman is constantly searching for her freedom and such freedom varies with tradition, religion, and politics.

Likewise, the Spanish director Pedro Almodóvar specializes in representing similar themes. Almodóvar's women are ordinary, marginalized, but also chaotic – and it is through the muddle of their lives that he weaves empathetic and complex representations of women. It is interesting because Almodóvar is a man, which brings us back to the subject we started with in this section: *perspective*. I still believe, as argued hitherto, storytelling does not require that only a black woman can make a film about black women. Nor does it demand a female Muslim director to produce a film about Muslim women. What is significant is the need to empathize with class interests of our subjects, and then generate cooperative representations that are diverse in their voices. As such, perhaps the issue of sexuality should be raised here, in the sense of questioning whether or not marginalized perspectives are better able to access other marginalized perspectives. As Bonny Cassidy asks, 'Does Almodóvar's homosexuality provide another layer of "access" to the complexity of his female characters, simply by virtue of bringing a marginal lens?'

Through recommending some of these conscientious films to our students and encouraging class discussions about their themes, critical pedagogy can conscientize students on how best to capture and articulate women's voices. An increasing number of subject generated representations are providing an opportunity for women to speak up and challenge oppressive and patriarchal institutions and systems. In this case, we want our students to examine what constitutes voice and how media platforms allow for the amplification of that voice. For example, some social structures might not allow women to speak in traditional public spheres. Yet these women do speak.

Think of the old body of women advisors who sit with traditional male leadership as they adjudicate cases in these traditional or customary courts. The women listen attentively and silently, and then in private, advise the leaders of their assessment, which usually informs how those leaders resolve the conflicts at hand. My mother might not have spoken up in these spheres. Yet I remember in the evenings when we ate with my father, he would narrate a conflict that was playing itself out in the court of the men's public sphere. My mother would listen and then analyse the issue for him. He would, days later at the men's forum, appear very wise in regurgitating the same advice from mother, likely without acknowledging her. Now the question is: whose voice is it? My mother's or father's? What it shows is that even in patriarchy, women find those imperceptible spaces in which they contest hegemony.

My friend Julie Bernardo adds that it is preferable for women to be able to speak directly in society on issues that ultimately include or affect them, yet women have always played a strong role in directing society from the sidelines, and in essence this is still the case today. Bernardo further observes that in any society, particularly where most people – men or women – are unable to argue directly for themselves, people are continually having to come up with imaginative ways to contend from the sidelines and probably always will ... This may not be ideal, but it is reality, whether we care to admit it or not. Representing these women's marginalized experiences and how they have had to live them requires that we learn to listen to alternative voices. Bonny Cassidy observes that if we are accustomed to hearing dominant voices speaking, we might not be trained to listen for the voices that are talking more quietly at the edge. What if they 'speak' differently? What if they don't 'speak' at all, but use a different sort of expression? Can we learn and teach how to better be alert to these signs (and to when they might be obscured)?

The main takeaway from this section is that teachers of critical pedagogy have the moral and epistemological responsibility to expose students to critical representations in films, radio, photography, and more. The aim is to illustrate that although most social structures have undermined the presence and voice of women in public polities, there are times and spaces in which women do speak. We should also be able to demonstrate to students that in some representations, what is important is the authenticity of the voice in question, even if we do not like the messenger. The authenticity of representations of women can only be measured by the ability to pay attention to the class issues faced by the women in question. As our students are introduced to critical films, exhibitions, photography or music on and about women, let us challenge them to think of some of these issues: Why is it important to have a female author or producer or director? Would the story have been different if someone other than a woman produced the representations? How can a man acquire a woman's perspective? Could we assume that the depicted women are strong? What can we learn from their struggles?

Colonial feminism to southern feminism

Not all western feminism is colonial. Yet, the *universalization, secularization*, and *modernization* of western feminism is very much evident in the way western media and polity treat the clothing and dressing of the other. The *niqaab, haik* or *burqa* for example have often been construed as indices of oppression in traditional societies, the societies that Daniel Lerner (1958) expected to be modernized. The writer Frantz Fanon (1965) foresaw this cultural struggle when he warned in the 1960s of the serious contestations over the representation of southern women. Fanon observed that efforts towards 'unveiling' these oppressed Arab women would become an occupation of western institutions and interests.

In a similar vein, Spivak, Mohanty, Djebar, and many southern feminists demonstrate that western (and often, white bourgeoisie) women in senior leadership positions are presented as a symbol of freedom and modernity. In contrast, most women in Muslim countries such as Saudi Arabia who have not been permitted to drive until recent legal reforms, have been presented as being stuck in traditional primitivity. Deepa Kumar offers an interesting analysis of how western media is implicated in constructing these contrasts even with limited understanding of the progress that these 'backward' countries have made over the years. Western media disputes the alternative and empathetic version put forth by southern experts, despite these western media experts having never visited or lived in these southern countries (Kumar, 2014).

What Kumar is arguing here regards the problem of *generalization of singularities* and how experiences of cases in one or two Muslim countries are postulated by the media to imply that they are representative of *all* Muslim countries. In a video on *Orientalism*, Said recalls how, in the aftermath of the 1995 Oklahoma bombing, the media and punditry were already defining the explosion as having a 'Middle Eastern trait', when in reality the terrorist was a white American – Timothy McVeigh (Palestine Diary, 2012). Thence, two attributes of colonial feminism stand out. First is the centrality of the western state as a 'liberator', notwithstanding its repressive and violent actions that hurt the very southern women it is supposed to liberate. Kumar (2014) describes the 'historical weaknesses' of western liberal feminism as being racist and patronizing towards southern women and women of colour who are perceived as victims rather than subjects and agents of their own change. Political leaders such as Angela Merkel, Margaret Thatcher, and Hillary Clinton are seen as strong feminists, even when they have used violent military intervention that eventually oppressed southern women. For Kumar (2014), the 'US women cannot achieve their liberation on the bodies of the victims of the empire by raining bombs', after all, the 'empire does not liberate, it subjugates'. Think also of the female US Army officers at Abu Ghraib Prison in Baghdad who tortured prisoners and celebrated next to the victims' bodies.

The second aspect of colonial feminism concerns the centrality of media discourse in normalizing violence, including female violence perpetrated in the name of the empire. Liberalism is postulated as an emancipatory intervention that aims to achieve a society that is equal, democratic, and just. After all, it is assumed that the East aspires to become the West (Lerner, 1958). This thirst for violent modernity is replicated in popular media. Kumar observes that 'shows such as *Homeland* reproduce imperialist feminism not only through its plot line and female lead character, Carrie Mathison, but also through its ad campaigns' (Kumar, 2014).

Mahmood Mamdani (2007) also explores the media's role in justifying western military and often violent interventions, defining it as 'the politics of naming'. He argues that though Iraq and Darfur have similar conflicts, they are 'named' differently by western media and experts, which has resulted in calls for intervention forces in Sudan, even when the same intervention has literally destroyed the peace that was there in Iraq. Likewise, bell hooks (1994:3) discusses how naming 'affords those in power access to modes of communication that enable them to project an interpretation or a description of their work, actions, etc. that may not be accurate, that may obscure what is taking place'.

Such a 'politics of naming' results in many consequences, one of which is the failure to see the actual perpetrators of the violence that occurs in the global South. Often the perpetrators are painted as male, and in the process, it becomes near impossible to see the agency of female perpetrators. *Masculine violence calls for masculine counter-violence.* The experience from the global South demonstrates that the root of violence is patriarchy – yet patriarchy does not necessarily have to have a penis. In fact, there is evidence pointing to examples of patriarchal violence that is nurtured and sustained by women. *Patriarchal violence has a vagina too.*

Since 2001, the US government has launched a global war on terror that has turned the world upside down. Iraq and Syria, which were once relatively stable, are frontlines of a bloody civil war. As a central sign and signifier in the vocabulary of *the view from here*, western humanism, with its own language orthodoxy and all its false sense of sincerity, empathy, and care, becomes an opportunity to instil and perform public acts of forgetting about the evils that the empire is actually guilty of. Such colonial violence has women at its heart too, which seems progressive from a western perspective, but not from a southern perspective. Our role as students of society is to expose this oppressive regime of violence inherent in colonial feminism.

Celebrating southern feminisms

The global South is no longer here nor there. Because of migration and other reasons, many southern feminists are writing from the global North. As such, southern feminism is not necessarily about the location of the authors – it is about the perspective they bring to feminism. Saba Mahmood (2005: 25) contends that there is an aspect of southern feminism that seems to 'occupy an uncomfortable place' in feminist *praxis*. Such feminism advances 'practices and ideals embedded within a tradition that has histori-cally accorded women a subordinate status' (Mahmood, 2005: 25). What it means is that the various stages of southern feminisms that are gradually transforming traditional and patriarchal societies are never acknowledged in colonial feminism. In Egypt for example, Mahmood carried out an anthropo-logical study of the women's mosque movement, which has become a feature of the Islamic Revival that started in the 1970s in the Islamic world.

The women's mosque movement would first emerge in homes when women 'started to organize weekly religious lessons', the aim being to advance their reading of the Quran, the Hadith, and associated exegetical and edificatory literature (Mahmood, 2005). Because of this, though the mosque movement may be criticized for being apolitical due to its focus on piety, it is nevertheless contributing to the transformation of 'many aspects of social life' such as dress styles, speech standards, entertainment, home economics and management, social welfare for the poor, and the opening up of public debate (Mahmood, 2005). What this shows is that to understand the nature and role of southern feminism, particularly in very traditional and religious societies, studies must take on ethnographic approaches and try to understand feminist agency as manifested in strengthening female consciousness and politics. After all, female agency might not be openly transformative based on western standards, but nevertheless, it is gradually contributing to what Michel Foucault described as the *parrhesia*: the rupturing of citizen voices, which are implicated in the generation and contestation of power.

Women in development

This is a significant area because some of the world's great socio-economic challenges do emanate from the lack of recognition of the fundamental role played by women in socio-economic development. While certain designated holidays such as International Women's Day provide an opportunity to reflect and celebrate the contribution of women, teachers of critical pedagogy can cultivate spaces in their teaching to conscientize their students on this. There are three significant areas in which western feminism attempts to monopolize the discourse around female empowerment; these three notions are – and not necessarily in order of importance – *the dress, the kitchen*, and *the uterus*.

The dress

The first concerns civilizing the traditional woman, and it begins with transforming the way they dress. It is well documented that women grow much of the world's food, working and nurturing the land and the environment; they raise families; they are major contributors to the informal economy even when they are largely financially excluded. These women are also the backbone of public and private life within traditional societies. Yet at the same time, women experience the worst forms of structural violence and marginalization. Excluded from much of the formal economy, subjugated under some traditional governance systems, assaulted and harmed during violent conflicts, women seem to be stuck at the bottom of the socio-economic totem pole.

For western development interventions, rescuing this 'brown woman' becomes one of the first necessary steps in the project of modernizing the other. In the aftermath of Beijing 1995 (the Fourth World Conference on Women), the problematic *women in development* paradigm attempted to celebrate the existence of this independent woman. Gender and feminism were seemingly conflated and very much associated with economic empowerment of women as a prerequisite to total transformation and independence. Organizations would develop and deliver micro-credit and financial inclusion programmes to ensure women achieved and enjoyed independence from men. In fact, men were seen as vestiges of patriarchy and structural violence.

Yet alongside this endeavour was another more ideologically sinister project at work. In *A Dying Colonialism*, Fanon (1965: 38) observes in the chapter 'Algeria Unveiled' that the woman wearing the traditional veil was represented as 'humiliated, sequestered, and cloistered'. Development interventions were meant to rescue this oppressed woman, because after all, this traditional woman had numerous possibilities awaiting her future if only she could be rescued from the structural violence perpetrated by men. For Fanon the traditional veil became a major battlefront for the liberation of this traditional woman. The assumption was, by rescuing this woman, it would become easier to liberate the men and the patriarchal systems. This attempt is what Fanon describes as the 'bone of contention in a grandiose battle', a contestation of symbolic power of colonial intervention in the south. The place of conservative religion in modernity is currently being hotly debated in American and European polity.

While policy and legislation can be employed to eradicate such injustices, this chapter proposes that carefully planned transformative education will provide a platform for a moral *conscientization* among development practitioners so that they begin to celebrate the women they have known, such as their mothers to great-grandmothers, sisters to aunties, mentors to friends. The aim should be to celebrate them not for how they are contributing to western civilization, but how they are exercising collective agency in gradually shaping the religious and traditional polity in the global South. In such pedagogy, the focus is on celebrating the women-led leadership in advocating for the realization of their full potential and capabilities. Yet it must be emphasized, that in engaging in this kind of pedagogy, cultural values that celebrate women – even if they do not speak to the idealistic notions of western civilization – are very much relevant and should be promoted. Fanon recognized the traditional garb worn by women as being key to their playing a critical role in the fight against colonialism. Yet the colonial French institutions would plan to 'unveil' and thus civilize such women. The implicit assumption therefore is that all women must look the same, and thereby 1) assimilate to empire; and 2) more specifically, assimilate to a distinct set of sexualized signs made through the discourse of clothing.

The kitchen

A second important phenomenon is the place of the kitchen in a woman's life. Again, there seems to exist some space in western polity that assumes the kitchen is a prison, that over and above whatever responsibility a woman has in the home, she is not traditionally the cook. In fact, the notion of the woman as a mother and a nurturer of life and family is being undermined and rejected under teachings and discourses that are against the religious and cultural values of most southern traditions. We should remember that in western modernity, traditions are a form of backwardness, unless they can be modified.

In the western world this may be the case, for several reasons. One is that the traditional family unit is changing in shape or is being constantly modernized. In many arrangements, a family is no longer a man and a woman. Two, could be the fact that the notion of family headship as a man's responsibility is being constantly questioned. We see an increased sharing of financial responsibility, where the man and woman split the rent, utility bills, and mortgage premiums. To cook therefore is no longer necessarily associated with a woman, as more and more men enter and occupy the kitchen space comfortably.

In the majority of the global South, and of course in rural and regional areas of the global North, the kitchen is, and has always been, the space for the woman. Before we embark on an exogenous criticism of the moral validity of the kitchen as a 'woman's space', we should remember that in such communal settings where the public and private spaces are occupied by males and traditional leadership, the kitchen becomes a sanctuary that offers the woman privacy to perform her citizenship without male interference. And it is in the sanctity of that kitchen that women share secrets, share knowledge about a host of things including traditional love concoctions and potions (to domesticate their husbands) or how to care for the woman's body, how to deal with difficult husbands, sexual and reproductive health, or even stories about death, puberty, and life.

And the kitchen is not just a space within the main house. Often a kitchen is a separate building from the main dwelling. It is where food harvests are kept, where chickens and other animals are kept, as well as equipment for working on the farm. As we grew older, some of my siblings and I were made to move out of the main house and sleep in the kitchen, probably to function as watchmen granted the food bank the kitchen was. And if women had anything they wanted to keep secret from anyone, especially their husbands, this was the space. Utensils such as bamboo baskets, water pails, drinking cups, and the like would be stored here. And as girls grow older, mothers, aunties, and grandmothers would sit here and provide advice on sexual and reproductive health, on being a woman, and why it was important to look after one's family.

The point being: there are parts of the world where a woman grows up looking forward to getting married and making her husband happy. Yet there are strands of western and southern feminism that dismiss such aspirational values as overly traditional and unmodern, and that they should be abandoned for western values. Postcolonial thinking however demonstrates that we live in a multipolar world with multiple centres and values. Values of respect, empathy, and love towards women can still be exercised for women whose goal is to raise families and look after their children and husbands.

The uterus

The third phenomenon concerns the uterus, both in its material and symbolic forms. Even if there are variations to the debates around the world, the central tenet from the perspective of western feminism is that a woman has the sole right to decide on what she does with her body. Whoopi Goldberg reaffirms this individual right in *The View* (2018) television programme in the aftermath of the news that Justice Anthony Kennedy was retiring from the US Supreme Court. Goldberg expressed her fears that Kennedy's replacement would overturn the famous 1973 Roe v. Wade US Supreme Court decision, something that would happen in 2022 (Totenberg and McCammon, 2022). Goldberg emphasized that 'I am trying to hold on to my personal rights, so that you can have the right you want' and that anyone who does not agree with that better 'get out of my behind, get out of my vagina' (*The View*, 2018).

In much of the global South, the various forms of communitarian ideals that emphasize the role of the community in safeguarding family life means that there are forces that determine who marries who, when they get married, with what dowry, and that they should have children. From the perspectives of western modernity, such communitarian ideals may seem incoherent, yet the reality is that individuality in these places is expressed through community values. There is nothing like an individual who makes sole decisions even regarding their own bodies without the mediation of the community. In the case of traditional women, the uterus can be both liberating and oppressive.

In the case of my mother, the uterus greatly oppressed her at first, because she could not initially bear children. For some reason within most of these patriarchal frameworks, women experience infertility. So, one or two of her husbands ran away. My name is actually a verb, Tulinje, meaning to try. My father came along, and told my mother, 'Let's try', and eventually I was born, followed by three wonderful sisters who I love very much. My mother's uterus was thus both her prison and her liberation. A prison because, in traditional settings, it is expected that a woman will bear children. And if she cannot, traditional corrective procedures, including visiting traditional healers, should be explored. Having children for any woman is a great privilege; an honour that cannot easily or casually be passed over. Reproduction and procreation are at the centre of traditional and religious polity.

The point is, while not having children is a woman's right in neoliberal feminist politics, it is equally a traditional woman's right to desire bearing children and to celebrate and identify with that – so much so that from a southern perspective, a woman without a child is considered not fully realized. The ability of the uterus to perform reproductive capabilities is immaterial; the perceptions and attitudes towards its functionality are pertinent. Likewise, a rite of passage is central in many traditional societies, the very societies that western modernism fantasizes about westernizing. Upon reaching puberty, boys and girls are taken for initiation. Central to this education is how to care for the body of the member of the opposite sex.

Upon reaching marriage age in whichever relevant local context, it is often the uncles or aunties that play a leading role as adjudicators in ensuring smooth ceremonies. They are there to organize the dowry payment, the engagement ceremony, and, where and when necessary, the wedding ceremony. In most of these instances, a man and woman will be forbidden to cohabit if they are not married, even if they wanted to, after all, society does not tolerate such behaviour. Perhaps with increasing modernization in the cities and capitals of the global South, increasing numbers of unmarried couples are cohabiting.

What it means is that, yes, an individual does have rights, but these rights are mediated by the community. Generally speaking, no matter how strongly a person feels romantically about any partner, they will not go ahead and marry them without 'permission' from their immediate or extended family. It otherwise becomes a problem if there is an illness or death of one of the partners or any children born thereof, because the community will be reluctant to provide support largely due to such a union remaining 'unrecognized', and hence, 'invisible' or 'inauthentic'.

All these three tenets – dress, kitchen, uterus – lead us to a critical factor regarding this new woman that is posited as an example of valour, strength, and civilization. This is the woman who will stand up for herself, speak for herself, and as it appears in some of the western discourses, will not forgive if her rights are violated or if she is wronged. One of the two major orthodox discourses that has emerged out of the recent feminist praxis in the west, the #MeToo movement, is that during any sort of election, a 'true' woman cannot support a man especially if there is a female candidate standing against him. Yet there are grey areas and nuances one cannot ignore.

A pedagogy of women

In the society in which I grew up, women have always been the first to wake up in the morning. By doing so, they launch the new day. They set the tasks of the day: the men go to the fields, the children journey to collect firewood. I would be sent to the market to sell farm produce if it was not during the school term. The women organize the work on the farms, particularly smallholder farms. They will cook the food, and if it is not available, they tend to look for it. Sometimes, they have to combine domestic chores with informal labour so that they can be paid in corn flour or rice, which they use to prepare the main dish. As such, in the global South, it is the women, and not the clock, that tell the time.

On the balance of work and responsibility, this would seem from Mill's (1859: 1) perspective, a kind of 'subordination of one sex to the other'. These 'existing social relations between the two sexes' are conceived to be 'wrong' as they offer power and privilege to one sex, and hence require addressing. In terms of the correction, western liberal feminism proffers theories and strategies that aim to seek to replace this imbalance with 'a principle of perfect equality that doesn't allow any power or privilege on one side or disability on the other' (Mill, 1859/2017: 1). Such 'subordination' thesis is accompanied by two suppositions. The first one is that in these instances, 'men have a right to command, and women an obligation to obey'. The second, is that women are denied any 'freedom or privilege that is rightly allowed to men' (Mill, 1859/2017: 1).

There are many contexts in which women are subordinated to men, however, opportunities exist where women carve out liminal spaces in which they exercise independence and subordination to no one but themselves. Let us take the custom of menstruation for example. The rules and regulations governing how women and men behave during menstruation might have been set up by male-dominated decision-making structures. In these societies, a menstruating woman is unclean, and is prohibited from undertaking certain public and household chores. In the home, she might be advised against cooking, or seasoning the stew with salt or serving food and water to the husband. In villages and communities where sanitation facilities are almost non-existent, there is perhaps a public health rationale to this. Men are advised against sleeping with women during this time; cautioned not to drink water from a pail that has a cooking stick placed at its mouth (the notice women use to inform husbands they are menstruating). There are cases of women placing the cooking stick over the pail of drinking water longer than anticipated, punishing husbands by denying them sex. After all, no man is expected to be counting days or questioning the woman about an extended menstruation cycle – the traditional initiation places emphasis on leaving women alone when menstruating. Critical feminist literature demonstrates how women employ their bodies as articles of resistance in speaking against oppressive social structures.

Granted this aforementioned discussion, how do development practitioners integrate feminism, especially southern feminism, in their praxis? This section offers six lessons on how best development practitioners of the field can address the question of women in their endeavours:

First, development practitioners of the field should ideally, where possible, be paired with female practitioners when entering or working within communities. Some cultures are highly sensitive to gender dynamics, to such an extent it is considered improper for a married woman for example to speak with a male unknown to her.

Second, development practitioners should, whatever issue they are working on, begin with community mapping which also includes mapping women and their activities. Who are the women here? What are their ages? Education? What do they do? What is their general experience? What are the key customs and traditions affecting women?

Third, speak alongside women. City-minded practitioners – including female ones – sometimes have problems understanding and communicating with rural and regional women, women with less education, and women struggling financially who appear backward-looking. Speaking with these women involves studying them, listening to their stories without judgement, joining them in their daily activities – and that is why having female partners during such exercises is vital, especially in places where gender sensitivities are high.

Fourth, ensure the presence and participation of women in meetings and sessions. It should be emphasized to development practitioners to develop local instruments that record meeting attendance and participation: How many people attended the meeting? How many were women? How many women spoke? How many women contributed to debates on critical issues? What was the kind of involvement?

Fifth, it is imperative we collect and catalogue women's songs and performances, as these will become critical when developing interventions. What songs do they sing? What performances do they perform? Is such a performance for everyone?

Sixth, we should develop an analytical framework on women and power in the local community. Who are the powerful women? What gives them power? How did they attain it? All this becomes useful as we begin to think of the web of local development, and the nodal junctures where women can play a critical part.

There is growing pressure on teachers, educators, and curriculum developers to consider introducing and exposing students to alternative theories, views, and paradigms on women. This chapter has attempted to emphasize the role development practitioners play in consolidating feminist practice and perspectives during deliberative development. Development practitioners of the field need to open their eyes to *see and hear women*. Women might not be allowed to drive in one conservative country, but that should not mask our ability to see that some of these countries have produced female leaders – something most civilized countries of the west have struggled to achieve. Or a woman might not speak at a public meeting, but that does not mean that her community does not acknowledge women's perspectives. A major argument is the idea that we can teach development practitioners to listen to women, to understand and respect them outside the intellectual confines of western feminism. In teaching about women and feminism, it is imperative that we allow for diversity of perspectives to flourish. There are other ways of celebrating and making sense of women beyond colonial feminism.

Notes

1. Wikipedia (2022) 'Negro Project' [online] <https://en.wikipedia.org/wiki/Negro_Project> [accessed 15 August 2022].
2. I am thankful to Julie Bernardo and Bonny Cassidy for enriching my thoughts in this chapter.

CHAPTER 5

On forgiveness and trauma

Theatre in the age of trauma

This chapter builds on the South African director John Kani's uses of theatre to facilitate a collective discourse on forgiveness and reconciliation in post-apartheid South Africa. My assumption is that theatre directors especially within the protest and workshop tradition are also development practitioners. The discussion seeks to challenge development practitioners of the field on how they work and engage with groups and communities that are hurting, experiencing trauma, and that have no trust in governance systems. Experiences of colonization and violence impact the quality of participatory democracy and deliberative development by creating a host of problems. Principal among which is the lack of popular trust in the institution of the state and its associated governance systems.

For example, Australia's NSW Department of Community Services (2009) observes that for communities that have experienced violent colonization, as in the case of Indigenous peoples, there is mistrust of development institutions and the prevalence of grief and loss. Likewise, Nesrine Malik (2001) argues that the rejection of or hesitancy to the Covid-19 vaccine worldwide should be understood in the context of people losing faith in the state. This makes it imperative to have a different kind of organic intellectual to mediate postcolonial development dialogues and bring people into the framework of deliberative development. The overall aim is to assuage people's documented and undocumented pain.

The pain being discussed here is a kind of continuum, oscillating between individual pain and collective pain (as experienced by black people under apartheid). Evidence suggests that violence breeds grief, loss, and trauma, which often breeds a host of health inequalities. These range from 'mental health issues, self-harm and intentional injury, suicide, drug and alcohol misuse and addiction, over-representation in the juvenile and criminal justice systems, over representation in welfare systems, homelessness, family and domestic violence, general feeling of hopelessness, relationship/connection breakdown, loss of identity' (NSW Department of Community Services, 2009:6).

It does not make sense therefore to discuss development with traumatized communities who have not yet dealt with their loss and pain. And what this chapter then asks is the critical question: How do people forgive so that they are able to contribute to the reconstructions of themselves and of their communities? And more specifically, how does a development field staff, or practitioner of the field contribute to this process? As if responding to this very conundrum during an interview with Al Jazeera about his 2002 play, *Nothing But the Truth*, John Kani examines questions of post-apartheid pain, trauma, and the Truth and Reconciliation Commission (TRC):

> *I was absolutely in favour, total support [for the TRC]. But when it comes to the individual, to myself, I could not answer this question: do I forgive? In 1985, my younger brother was shot. He was a poet. They used to recite their poems at political rallies, at funerals and cultural events. While attending a funeral of a nine-year old girl killed during the riots, he was reciting a poem. And the police dispersed the crowd [shots were fired] and my younger brother was killed. The years went by and I carried the anger, the bitterness, the want for revenge. [And when Mandela and Tutu introduced the TRC] I embraced it whole-heartedly. But with me, the question I could not understand, nor answer was the question of forgiveness when no one has come forward to ask you to say forgive me ... I opened the play on 4th July 2002 ... I finally reconciled within myself, I found the power of forgiveness that healed me, and that the perpetrator, or the other party in this forgiving business was irrelevant ... So that was the power of it. Without that process, I do not believe RSA would be where it is today. We needed to confront that past, we needed to be given the opportunity to pour out that anger. We also needed to hear from the other side, because we needed to know who killed who ... to bring closure ... to focus on the reconstruction* (Al Jazeera, 2007).

Kani's use of theatre as a process for 'confronting that past' contributes to the ongoing dialogue and project of reconciliation in South Africa. But most importantly, theatre became a therapeutic facility for exploring hidden and buried pain. South Africa's premier theologian and Nobel Peace Prize Laureate, Bishop Desmond Tutu, documented the painful exposure to domestic violence. Recalling his childhood where he 'helplessly' experienced his father physically and emotionally abusing his mother, Tutu discusses the 'hopeless despair' of witnessing people we care about 'hurting each other in incomprehensible ways' (Tutu, 2014). Tutu (2014) observed 'how difficult the process of forgiving truly is', particularly knowing that even though his mother did not 'deserve the pain that was inflicted on her', his father 'caused pain because he himself was in pain'. For Tutu, forgiveness becomes difficult because the pain does not go away – in fact, 'the traumas we have witnessed or experienced live on in our memories. Even years later, Tutu confesses, they can cause us fresh pain each time we recall them'. So what is forgiveness, and how does a development practitioner build trust with people so that they are able to lead conversations on and about local development?

Discussions of forgiveness are, according to Alex Clark (2018), 'complex and personal', largely because if we 'set the bar for casting miscreants into the outer darkness too low, we risk the isolation of perfectionism; if we set it too high, we might find ourselves seething with suppressed resentment'. How should development teachers and practitioners understand these complex debates on forgiveness? How do they embrace the various perspectives, including non-western and indigenous perspectives on looking at forgiveness? This chapter is not a discussion of a list of things and issues that should or should not be forgiven, for that depends on personal and collective circumstances. Apartheid was a crime against humanity, yet there were individual families who suffered more than others. While the Truth and Reconciliation Commission headed by Bishop Tutu tried to offer wrong doers the opportunity to ask for forgiveness and the wronged families to understand what had actually happened, it all depended on the individual suffering families to decide to forgive. The truth is: a blanket admission of guilt could not have assuaged the personal and familial trauma suffered.

Theatre, just like other forms of artistic expression, provides the space to examine how violence has destroyed lives and civilizations, and critically, how people remember those experiences. Kani's work in using theatre to explore forgiveness follows a long and established tradition of art being employed to advocate for peace and harmony. Pablo Picasso would use his art to denounce violence, and thus in a way, contributed to critical dialogues on how best to remember the past. His most memorable piece in regard to this was *Guernica*, a 'wrenching reflection on the devastating bombardment in April 1937 of the Basque village of Guernica during the Spanish Civil War' (Grovier, 2019). The violence of war and the crimes against humanity that are often swept under the rug would also become key features of Picasso's art. Kelly Grovier (2019) observes that in response to serious allegations of atrocities committed by US troops in the Sinchon Massacre, Picasso, in *Massacre in Korea*, depicted a 'group of women and children about to be slaughtered at point-blank range by a faceless gang of robotic goons'. At this time when Picasso prompted others to confront the violence of war and how it destroys innocent lives, it was a reminder of 'Francisco de Goya's famous painting *The Third of May 1808* (1814), whose choreography of sinister soldiers mowing down defenceless civilians is conceived along exactly the same theatrical lines' (Grovier, 2019).

Over the years, the horrors of war have been explored through music, song, dance, and art. In Lebanon, refugee NGOs are helping refugee children who have escaped the Syrian conflict to process their trauma through drawing (Stoughton, 2017). As observed by Al Jazeera's India Stoughton (2017):

> *Myra Saad, the founder and director of Artichoke Studio, a registered art therapy centre in Beirut, said that it tends to follow a series of steps common to different branches of psychotherapy: 'one, to have a safe space where you can express yourself; two, to become more aware of what you're feeling and where it's coming from; and three, to eventually change'. The primary goal is to give participants 'the space and time to be children again', Saad told Al Jazeera.*

What these foregoing experiences show is that art is a transformative instrument for community engagement, particularly in contexts where individuals and groups have experienced horror and trauma, often resulting from oppressive or bad governance. After all, 'there is much to be angry about, and there are many perpetrators of cruelty and malfeasance to confront', argues Clark (2018). This chapter however acknowledges that art might likely bring perpetrators of evil to justice. *Might*. But it often doesn't. In fact, there is a danger of art opening old wounds and trauma that victims were working to overcome. Yet as John Kani observes, art such as theatre enables sufferers and victims 'to confront that past', offering an opportunity for people to register and pour out righteous anger.

The theatre of forgiveness

The question is, where do we begin to forgive? As Derrida (1997: 27) observes, 'there is no limit to forgiveness, no measure, no moderation, no "to what point?"' Without focusing on what can and cannot be forgiven, Clark (2018) reminds us, 'we can derive something of great potential value from the idea that we are, as human beings, capable of setting the past aside'. Even in the age where it is becoming popular and acceptable, especially in the age of social media, to 'encourage the discourse of denunciation, in which a person's transgressions co-exist with their present lives, in which the line between "calling out" and futile zero-sum bullying is ever blurrier, is not, ultimately, a pathway to happiness'. After all, as Clark (2018) observes, research does point to the 'reparative power of admitting our imperfections, saying sorry and moving forward'.

In western modernity, forgiveness has been historically associated with both governance and accountability on the one hand, and religious expression of faith on the other. Derrida attempts to explore the definition of forgiveness in terms of measuring what it is really for. He defines it as 'an act' and also a 'theatre' (Derrida, 1997: 27, 28). He acknowledges the religious undertones that accompany the term, whose act and theatre has increased in the cosmopolitan world with institutions, individuals, and communities asking for forgiveness. Derrida (1997) observes that forgiveness is associated with other acts such as expressing regret for past or recent behaviour or actions, confession, seeking penance and repentance, apologising, and other similar behaviours. It is in this context that the role of performances becomes critical in helping groups and communities come face-to-face with the cultures of violence they have experienced.

As observed by Lea Harris of the US-based community wellness programme, PEERS (Peers Envisioning and Engaging in Recovery Services), 'theatre-based therapeutic programmes can help people of all ages to feel seen and heard, to raise awareness for change, and to explore and respond to challenging material onstage in a safe and supportive environment' (Harris, 2019). PEERS programmes and resources aim at reaching out to the most marginalized groups of communities experiencing poor mental health as a result of their traumatic experiences. A major programmatic intervention is *Healing Arts* which offers participants a safe space to 'explore mental health and wellness through art', after all, it is well known that art facilitates healing and recovery by empowering group members to become resilient, to process pain and hurt, and express difficult emotions through various artistic and performative mediums (Harris, 2019).

In the same vein, theatre directors the world over are using theatre to explore deeper issues of terror and trauma experienced by human beings. By doing so from a place of safety, theatre becomes a process of processing traumatic experiences by engaging the larger human family to help survivors witness and confront such pain collectively (Bogart, 2001). Similarly, Nathan Singh introduces the conceptual framework for the *theatre of trauma* through which he 'directs plays about individuals, communities, and cultures processing trauma in very active and theatrical ways'. Singh (2017) emphasizes that he wants his audiences to 'witness the messy and complicated landscape of their own traumas', which can be both 'triggering' and 'ultimately healing'. The overall aim is transformative, so that artists and audiences 'will feel a deeper compassion for human suffering and understand where it comes from' (Singh, 2017).

The practice of using theatre to examine violence, trauma, and pain has its origins in classical theatre, especially Greek tragedies. The daughter of King Agamemnon and Queen Clytemnestra, Electra, is a central figure in creative works by Sophocles and, of course, Euripides. Both Agamemnon and his slave mistress Cassandra are murdered, probably in a conspiracy involving close family members. Discussing one of the many performances of Electra, this time at Court Theatre in Chicago, Nathan Singh (2017) discusses how Electra processes her pain and grief:

> *Electra comes in ... ravaged by the emotional pain of her father's death. The women of the chorus start off by telling her to curb her rage. They all witnessed the same gruesome murder of Agamemnon, but they try to justify Clytemnestra's actions so that they can move on. They are essentially telling Electra to get over her pain and live her life. She cannot do that. It is too deep, this wound. They echo 'Do not breed grief from grief' and 'Why do you always waste your life away in endless grief. Grief for the life of those long dead.' In return, Electra feels alive in her grief. Alive in her rage. Her PTSD has not knocked her down but given her strength and purpose.*

While this play demonstrates the process of grieving, it also, according to Singh, 'shows the very delicate line between madness and trauma', which both interrupt the way victims make sense of reality. Singh continues to argue that 'Electra's reality has been altered with her mother murdering her father', placing her in a state of madness – and yet her mother, Clytemnestra, has too had her reality conflicted by the experience of her husband, Agamemnon, murdering their other daughter, Iphigenia. For Singh (2017: 69), trauma seems highly 'cyclical'.

The issue of violence committed by family and community members is one that John Kani examines in his play, *Nothing but the Truth*. Unlike Electra where the issue of vengeance repeatedly arises, Kani uses this theatre of trauma to explore forgiveness, and the ever-contentious question of 'moving on'. Forgiveness is largely tied to a form of deliberateness, of consciousness, and of course a willingness on the part of an individual to do three things: To *remember* the past clearly and truthfully, to *review* such past and recent actions and behaviour, and consciously decide to *overcome* (and not overlook), or in the words of Clark (2018), 'to set the past aside' for the sake of moving forward. For Kani, whose brother was shot dead by apartheid forces, the Truth and Reconciliation Commission provided a space for the collective experience of remembering, reviewing, and overcoming trauma. He emphasizes the role of TRC in helping people in pain 'confront that past', to 'pour out that anger', and eventually to 'bring closure' and 'focus on the reconstruction' (Al Jazeera, 2007). All these decision points are fundamental towards this 'act' and 'theatre' of forgiveness, as it implies that we are aware of what we are forgiving. Why are these three factors important?

Firstly, to remember the past is a critical step towards the performance of forgiveness – whether it is private or public. Remembering does not only imply committing to memory but it also demonstrates that we are aware of what is at stake, particularly in regard to the width and depth of the hurt a certain act caused us or our family or community. So crucial, however, is remembering clearly and truthfully. Remembering is a product of memory, which is malleable and dependent on how facts have been recorded and documented. As such, to remember clearly means that we have done our best to understand the truth (and gravity) of what happened. This is critical because we do not want to discover new facts in the future to make us regret forgiving some actions and behaviours.

Secondly, to review such actions means we have had the time and opportunity to examine and reflect upon the events and issues reflexively. We will then be able to acquire a nuanced understanding of what actually happened, what went wrong, the circumstances that made other parties act in the ways they did, and critically, why we have decided to forgive above all other avenues open to us. Kani's use of theatre comes into consideration here. He discussed on Al Jazeera the launching of his play, *Nothing but the Truth*:

> *I opened the play on 4th July 2002. That evening in a small town, with an audience of about 60% black and 40% white with ages ranging, with a thunderous applause and tears, with screaming from me at the end of it, with all pouring out, I finally reconciled within myself, and I found the power of forgiveness that healed me, and that the perpetrator, or the other party in this forgiving business was irrelevant ... It was a public proceeding, and it healed a number of people ... So that was the power of it.*

Kani's public proceeding of acknowledging pain leads to the third factor, in which forgiveness entails taking a decision to 'set aside' a grievance – its legitimacy notwithstanding – and then focus on the future. This was the role that the TRC played in South Africa, and as Kani notes, 'Without that process, I do not believe South Africa would be where it is today.' It does not necessarily imply that we forget or remove from our memory; we can both forgive and remember, after all they are not mutually exclusive. 'Setting aside' means we want to open a platform for a new conversation about fresh possibilities. In the traditional court concept of 'Gacaca' in Rwanda, genocide suspects have been tried, thus enabling individuals and communities to find closure (Nsengiyumva, 2012). In this case, the aftermath of the genocide oppresses both the victim and the perpetrators.

Similarly, in *Pedagogy of the Oppressed*, Freire discusses oppression as dehumanizing for both the oppressor and the oppressed. Freire (1970: 44) argues that the 'great humanistic and historical task' of the oppressed is 'to liberate themselves and their oppressors' because oppressors are unable to liberate anyone. Perhaps in realizing this, and how easy it is for oppressed to become new oppressors, Nelson Mandela would commit to the creation of a democratic, non-racist, and non-sexist post-apartheid South Africa. One would be compelled to believe that he knew apartheid oppressed both black and white people, as it forced black people to behave and function like black people, and white people as white, thus dehumanizing both peoples. Collective and individual forgiveness entailed the recognition of this fact. This recognition would make those forgiving understand that even the gravest atrocities were committed by people who had been dehumanized by a system.

Another example of forgiveness as a conscious action that seeks to look ahead is Joyce Seipei, the mother of 14-year-old activist Stompie Seipei who was killed in 1989. Winnie Madikizela Mandela was suspected of having ordered members of the Mandela United Football Club to murder Stompie (SABC Digital News, 2018). Madikizela Mandela and the underground movement has considered Sempei of being an apartheid spy. During the Truth and Reconciliation Commission hearings, Joyce Seipei had an encounter with Winnie Madikizela Mandela and she decided to forgive not only Winnie but all who were involved in the murder of her son, largely because she realized that if she did not forgive, the anger was 'going to consume her' (SABC Digital News, 2018). Ms Seipei even attended Madikizela Mandela's funeral in 2018.

There are lessons about forgiveness that emerge from this example and which are elaborated in Derrida's work. Derrida (1997: 29) links forgiveness to memory and repentance, giving an example of the Nuremberg tribunal in the aftermath of the Second World War as a 'performative event' which allowed for seeking 'grand forgiveness'. The trial itself then became a 'grand scene of repentance' (Derrida, 1997: 29). What this means is that forgiveness is not necessarily tied to justice or retribution, but a pathway for a new beginning. In this case, when perpetrators refuse to acknowledge their role in perpetuating an injustice, a trial becomes that avenue for unpacking what actually happened, in order for the victims to understand and appreciate how much they were wronged. Victims need to know what it is they are forgiving.

Likewise, in Rwanda, traditional courts have provided an avenue for perpetrators of atrocities during the 1990s genocide to fully confess their crimes and seek forgiveness from victims. These traditional community courts have been known as *Gacaca*, and were established to 'clear the backlog of the genocide cases' and at the same time 'achieve truth, justice and reconciliation among Rwandans' (Nsengiyumva, 2012). In Mozambique, a similar exercise was executed at the end of a brutal civil war between Samora Machel's FRELIMO[1] government forces and the apartheid government-funded RENAMO rebels. Towards the end of the war, the FRELIMO government held public hearings where the defeated rebels confessed to the atrocities they had perpetrated, asked for forgiveness, and committed to a reintegration programme (AfroMarxist, 2009).

It must be noted that Derrida (1997) acknowledges the challenges and complexity of forgiveness when it comes to 'crimes against humanity' as this concept brings up questions and concerns of 'discourse and legitimation', especially where crimes, murders, and atrocities are committed during legitimate revolutions. What is worth noting is that individuals and groups have every right to review atrocities and wrongs they suffered and refuse to forgive. There are wrongs that cannot be forgiven, and this discussion is not about exploring the limits of such. What is interesting in Derrida's debate is this conditional aspect of forgiving, that forgiveness should be granted if it is requested. Derrida notes this tension.

There exists a kind of transactional tension between two forms of forgiveness: the *unconditional and infinite forgiveness* granted only to those who have been found guilty or those who do not ask for it, and the *conditional forgiveness* which results from a wrongdoer's repentance. This chapter is about building these tensions and debates into our pedagogy, so that development practitioners appreciate the moral, ethical, and political value of forgiving – not as a careless process of setting aside the past, but rather as a deliberate struggle to, in the words of Stompie Seipei's mother, Joyce Seipei, avoid 'having this thing, this anger eat one inside' (SABC Digital News, 2018).

What this chapter seeks to argue for in principle is the introduction to and emphasis of forgiveness as a perspective that our students need to take towards life, rather than approaching forgiveness as an act or as a performance. As a perspective, forgiveness allows us as individuals to take a conscious look at the wrong that has been inflicted on us. So how and why should the pedagogy of listening emphasize forgiveness as a perspective?

Chiefly, in a world where we are increasingly becoming multicultural, the learning and working space is likely to comprise people of various cultures, ethnicities, and orientations. As a result, differences will abound. It is imperative we engage with development practitioners with regards to their understanding of forgiveness, and perhaps by opening ourselves up, debate on those things that we felt we were wronged on, and how we were able to find the inner strength to move on.

Second, forgiveness allows us the opportunity to understand our own role – minute as it may seem – in the error that initiated the wrong perpetrated against us. (To be clear: this category refers to banal transgressions that have no bearing on the life or dignity of individuals.) We are not blaming the victim in doing this, rather, we are seeking not to view ourselves as holding a higher moral ground than other people.

Third, since to err is human, so too is forgiveness. We should remember that at a certain point we will have wronged, and we will wrong others, and forgiveness is positively sweet when it is granted. We appreciate such when we make grave mistakes that can cost us our jobs or freedom, and certainly we become appreciative when someone decides to 'set aside' such an error, hence offering us an opportunity to think carefully in the way we relate to others.

Fourth, forgiveness as a perspective allows for a minimizing of conflicts, especially where we forgive errors that even the perpetrator is oblivious to having committed. In this case, victims have decided to either write off the error or document it and raise it with the person(s) in question at an opportune time in the future. This approach allows for a peaceful resolution to differences and conflicts, making way for more nuanced and mature conversations on the things that went wrong.

These four aspects seem to come together in the indigenous notion of *kudziletsa*. This is more of a perspective or lifestyle that combines elements of forgiveness, peaceful engagement, and letting go. Of late, there seems to have emerged a growing culture of wokeness that has taken root in modern polity, in which people with unpopular and 'unacceptable' opinions are called out, humiliated, and, often, cancelled out. In the context of such social justice wars there is no room for negotiation of problematic positions. They demand errors be punished, which is not always the case within indigenous knowledge systems, as observed by Ayishat Akanbi (2018):

> The problem with wokeness is that it has robbed many people of compassion and replaced it with more superiority. Compassion and empathy are more paramount to any social movement, to any form of progress. Once you have compassion and empathy you can often see that you have a lot more in common with people than you do apart. And it's the system that we live in that forcefully tries to group us with our differences. What is radical is kindness, what is radical is under-standing. Arguing with each other isn't actually radical at all, it's very conformist.

For Akanbi, anger without reflexivity tends to be reactionary and negative, rather than focusing on how best to build a thing into something better. Akanbi emphasizes the power of nuances as they help with understanding interconnectedness of issues. This thought seems similar to the notion of *kudziletsa*. The notion of *kudziletsa* is a deep indigenous epistemology meaning, in the literal sense, to hold oneself back (from reacting thoughtlessly); at the philosophical level, it is about a life of kindness that forgives freely. The idea of *kudziletsa* does not necessarily entail one does nothing against evil. A good example perhaps, is Mahatma Gandhi's *Satyagraha:* a form of peaceful and non-violent resistance against political oppression. Yet whereas *Satyagraha* involves disobeying oppressive laws, as would Martin Luther King's civil rights movement in the US, *kudziletsa* does not involve confrontation with evil. It would thus not be a relevant strategy and approach for collective advocacy in political reforms.

Kudziletsa can be considered an epistemological framework and praxis of 'refusing to resist evil', not for the sake of permitting and enabling evil to flourish, but, in Freire's terms, as a way to provide space for wrongdoers to conscientize. In the Turkish movie *Winter Sleep* (directed by Nuri Bilge Ceylan, 2014), Necla asks her brother Aydin what he thinks of the notion of 'not resisting evil'. For Aydin it is as simple as thieves breaking into one's house and one doing nothing about it. Or, in fact he argues, it is to remain indifferent in the face of evil. Lost on Aydin is the epistemological framework that could inform people's daily behaviour. For Necla and of course Nihal (Aydin's wife), 'not resisting evil is much deeper'. It is about the refusal to have a direct struggle against evil. Rebuking her husband, Nihal unpacks Necla's thoughts: 'It is very clear what she is saying. If someone does me harm, a thief or someone, I do not resist and by doing so, stir his conscience.'

There is actually no free ride. In this case, the conscientization is the carrot, but the threat of severe punishment is the actual stick. In terms of *Kudziletsa*, the idea is that no matter how much a wrongdoer has wronged us, we should always leave the space for them to become our friends. In fact, forgiveness is an act of liberation. Not resisting to engage evil thus entails a pedagogy in which individuals and groups engage privately with institutions and processes that can liberate them. Jesus did not ask anyone to suffer in silence, rather he advised, in Romans 12: 18 that 'If it is possible, as much as depends on you, live peaceably with all men.' This means peaceful negotiations and lobbying are very much on the table. How those are conducted, depends.

Theatre as performative agency in forgiveness

At this juncture, I want to pay attention to the role of theatre in exploring pain, trauma, and forgiveness. The use of theatre as a facility for interrogating pain and forgiveness has a long history. Augusto Boal introduced the notion of theatre of the oppressed to describe the experiments he was facilitating through dialogues in Brazil's impoverished neighbourhoods as a way of bringing people together to solve local development problems. Epistemologically, theatre of the oppressed is very similar to Freire's pedagogy of the oppressed in that both use local discussion groups to conscientize local people about the nature of problems and how increased democratization of efforts empowers them with transformative solutions.

Like the theatre of the oppressed, protest theatre in South Africa became a potent political weapon for contesting and fighting against apartheid. The work of Gibson Kente, Athol Fugard, John Kani, Winston Ntshona, Mbongeni Ngema, and many workshop forms of theatre became a critical voice in exposing the violence of apartheid in South Africa. In fact, John Kani describes such theatre as a 'cultural AK47' (Al Jazeera, 2007). This use of theatre would years later be adopted by numerous NGOs to educate the masses on social development issues and has been termed theatre for development. In my view, theatre for development describes groups of performance methodologies and approaches that employ song, music, theatre, drama, and dance as a way of sensitizing and mobilizing communities to transform their lives and communities. The works of Robert Mshengu McLaren, Zakes Mda, David Kerr, and Chris Kamlongera have provided the theoretical framework through which this form of transformative theatre has been understood.

For Mda, this theatre is theatre of the people and takes many forms: agitprop, comgen, forum, dramaturgy, and participatory theatre. The central element is that because there are few external facilitators animating community dialogues and asking difficult questions, theatre is used together as a space and discourse to deconstruct painful experiences. In Kenya, Ngũgĩ wa Thiong'o employed community theatre as a postcolonial space, discourse, and weapon for critical examination of disillusionment regarding independence in Kenya. Perhaps responding to a local woman who asked him to provide local people with a liberating education, wa Thiong'o teamed up with Ngugi wa Mirii to workshop a participatory theatre production of *Maitu Njugira* (Mother Sing for Me), following another project, *Ngaahika Ndeenda* (I Will Marry When I Want), which was banned by the government in 1977.

Through these collective performances, wa Thiong'o focused on the transformative process of creating content with the people, to an extent that, Ingrid Björkman argues, the process of creating the play enabled the villagers to educate themselves (Manyozo, 2002). In this case, wa Thiong'o conceptualized theatre as an agency of examining the pain and trauma of colonialism and new-found independence, especially in realizing that the new black class is merely a replica of the former white masters. Thus, theatre for development in this Marxist case is one created by and for the people in their own language using their own emotional resources – which reflects Augusto Boal's (1993) concept of poetics of the oppressed. As a discourse, a weapon, and a forum, such theatre of the oppressed provides an egalitarian opportunity for people to understand their own oppression, but at the same time, make sense of their own pain and find healing. Critical themes of forgiveness are explored in the use of theatre for development.

There is power in forgiving. It is never a sign of weakness. As a cornerstone of love, forgiveness is an exercise of power. Forgiveness is the ability to find our own voice to confront errors committed, and having weighed the available facts, we choose to move on – not because the error or errors in question are not serious, they often are, hence the need for forgiveness, but as Joyce Seipei observed with regards to Winnie Mandela's implication in the murder of her son, anger would eat at one inside and end up destroying our being. Forgiveness is a force, an enabling force which allows victims to assume and assert control over historical development to their advantage.

Perhaps one illustration of forgiveness lies in a John Kani play, *Nothing But the Truth*, which examines questions of truth and reconciliation. Sixty-three-year-old Sipho is about to bury his brother Temba, who died in exile. Sipho's interactions with his daughter and niece reveal his hatred for his brother (who slept with Sipho's wife), and also reveal an unresolved hatred for white South Africans, who are still considered to have collectively benefited from apartheid. For Kani's play, the message is simple: 'truth and reconciliation is, a process that has to begin at home' (Billington, 2007).

In reviewing his play, Kani differentiates between forgiveness at the individual level and collective forgiveness, as was the case with the Truth and Reconciliation Commission in South Africa. He observes that such a Commission focused on forgiveness and reconciliation between white and black people as was emphasized by both Bishop Tutu and Nelson Mandela, who 'put a band-aid around the nation' and made us all say, 'we forgive each other'. Yet such collective forgiveness was, for Kani, 'not true' because copious individuals require counselling and therapy to deal with the emotional scars and wounds of apartheid (Friends of ShaXperience, 2014). What this means is that to forgive apartheid – a crime against humanity – the victims must learn to forgive errors and crimes perpetrated by neighbours and friends.

The consequence of apartheid on the collective psyche of South Africans was that neighbour turned on neighbour, and particularly in the townships there was a lot of what Fanon would define as horizontal violence. The example was community members who burnt each other after accusing one another of being apartheid spies or working with the enemy. In such cases pardoning people without forgiving them becomes necessary for national unity and reconciliation. Insincere as it may seem, collective forgiveness becomes a stepping-stone and a political facility towards achieving national peace. Yet Derrida (1997) makes a distinction between forgiving someone (the person responsible) and forgiving something (a crime, fault, wrong), which, in the case of post-apartheid South Africa, required doing both.

The idea of forgiving and its actual implementation especially at the individual level opens up opportunities to find the right voice with which to explain what has been experienced. Instead of being eaten from within by anger and depression, victims assume power within themselves so that they do not become double victims – victims of the original wrong, and also victims of rage and despair. The victims refuse to become oppressed under the yoke of unresolved issues and questions. Sadly, in many cases victims fail to, are unable to, or refuse to move on after experiencing wrongdoing.

Theatre of trauma, reconciliation, and forgiveness

Mellor et al. (2007) discuss the question of indigenous perspectives with regards to collective crimes committed against a population group. A key aspect of their argument, especially in the context of Australia, is that 'reconciliation requires both an apology and forgiveness' (Mellor et al., 2007: 11). For the authors, reconciliation in this case has to be driven by institutions, largely because the crimes were committed at a grand scale. In the case of Australia, the violence of colonialism comprises invasion and dispossession, forced assimilation and control of indigenous lives, social disintegration, economic marginalization, and cultural alienation (Mellor et al., 2007). This is very similar to South Africa, where colonialism resulted in apartheid, which formalized and naturalized the dispossession and marginalization of black and Indian populations. To achieve reconciliation in such contexts requires apology, forgiveness, and the deconstruction of inequalities that emerged from that violence and trauma. Genuine apology cannot be accompanied by an unwillingness to change the status quo. In this case, an apology is a praxis; it is something that is reflected in both words and deeds.

The complexity of trauma, apology, and forgiveness in postcolonial spaces such as South Africa, where the original violence was perpetrated within a complex web of legal and policy instruments, means that processing this trauma becomes a difficult task. This is particularly so in cases where crimes were committed by institutions, breeding either unilateral or negotiated forgiveness (Mellor et al., 2007). Unilateral forgiveness is present in many religious traditions, as elucidated by Jesus' words, 'Father, forgive them.' The idea is that our physical and spiritual well-being depends on a refusal to harbour ill-feelings against others. On the other side sits 'negotiated forgiveness', which is a form of accountability in itself, as there exists a dialogue between those who committed the wrong and those who were wronged. In the contexts where collective wrongs were committed over a long period of time, apologies are necessary – chiefly from those who never committed the wrongs but remain beneficiaries. Descendants of the victims also have obligations to receive these apologies. In this complex scenario, workshopped theatre can be used to examine these critical questions in a number of ways.

First, in cases where there is much public shame associated with the past perpetration of violence, theatre can be employed to request collective forgiveness; to express collective penance so as to signify what Derrida (1997: 28) described as the 'urgency of memory'. What theatre does, especially workshopped theatre, is provide a platform and mirror for an implicated society to see itself being represented, which enables it to have sincere dialogues about what actually happened, and how the victims would feel empowered if an apology were given. These crimes do not necessarily have to have been committed by the group seeking forgiveness – the group could simply be complicit through silence. The Catholic Church or sections of its branches, principally in Latin America, has on several occasions apologized for its silence during atrocities committed by military juntas in several countries.

The Church also offered a collective apology and expressed deep regret for the sexual crimes committed by several clergy and for not doing enough to protect others against them. In 2008 the then Australian Prime Minister, Kevin Rudd, offered an apology to the country's Indigenous peoples (Australian Government, 2008). Importantly, this sorry speech did not merely say 'sorry' to the Stolen Generations – it detailed the specific wrongs carried out against Australia's Indigenous peoples. As Derrida points out with regards to collective apologies, the Australian Apology acknowledges the reality of the past and thus emphasizes the recollection of historical facts. We 'reflect on their past mistreatment'. The Apology goes on to depict the specific mistreatment, the policies and laws, the removal of children from their families, the 'pain, hurt and suffering', and the breakdown of families involved, and thus 'resolves that the injustices of the past must never, never happen again' (Australian Government, 2008).

Second, theatre provides a space for understanding the complexity of justice, and that collective forgiveness does not necessarily result in the first step to finding justice. Or to put it more succinctly: collective penance and apology is not necessarily an admission of guilt. Collective penance can sometimes be opaque, particularly where perpetrators do not believe they actually committed the said atrocities. This is what Hannah Arendt grappled with in *The Banality of Evil* as she observed the trial of Adolf Eichmann, one of the main organizers of the Holocaust. She observed that collective crimes, notably crimes against humanity, are largely committed within socio-political systems and processes, yet in the case of the Holocaust trials after the Second World War, there was no system on trial. In discussing this 'fearsome, word-and-thought-defying banality of evil' Arendt understood that totalitarianism dehumanizes people, making them act out mundane actions that seem insignificant at the individual level, but collectively considered, contribute to the perpetration of heinous crimes.

In analysing Eichmann's denial of hating Jews and of having killed anyone, Arendt (1963) would argue in a controversial point that Eichmann's inability to speak against the systematic killing of Jews was 'connected with an inability to think'. This observation, which seemed to absolve perpetrators of individual responsibility, would launch what Amos Elon described in the introduction to his book *The Excommunication of Hannah Arendt* as a 'civil war'. Yet what is worth pointing out is that even when the German people and government were acknowledging the role their nation had played in the Holocaust, the actual perpetrators such as Eichmann expressed a seemingly clean conscience. What theatre does in these cases is use performances as public murals, where history is recorded for future generations to remember the pain and trauma exacted on members of the society. And in instances where there is a substantial backlog of cases, where victims will not see justice administered, theatre ensures that victims and their families will know what happened, which goes some way towards helping them find closure.

Third, theatre becomes a classroom, which educates people on the significance of individual and specific roles played in perpetrating violence and other forms of traumatic experiences. In fact, from Eichmann's testimony, some perpetrators might see their actions as being mundane, banal, and insignificant, and not directly related to the actual crimes. Yet the crimes were indeed committed, and theatre performances provide illumination on how certain actions and inactions led to the committing of crimes. It is important that workshop theatre participants understand that a man selling tools for sharpening knives and machetes might not see their involvement in genocide (indirect it might seem), yet their continued supply of the sharpening stones contributed to the genocide. Or that their inability to respond to the constant cries for help from young girls sexually assaulted by their close relation enabled those crimes. In these contexts, theatre creates a platform where participant perpetrators come to terms with the error of their ways and also understand the harm they have caused. By doing so they face the victims and their families, asking for forgiveness. This approach might seem at odds with international human rights law whose focus is on justice, as it involves a more reconciliation or restorative-type justice.

Some afterthoughts

Many societies in the global South have experienced pain, marginalization, and trauma as a result of colonization, capitalism, and globalization. There is a growing class of landless people without any safety net, without any hope of employment. Meanwhile, a growing culture of violence against women and other powerless groups is consolidating. More often than not, development field practitioners will find themselves in the field working and dealing with such traumatized communities. It requires a special skills and mentality set to be able to engage with these groups. What this chapter has pointed out is that groups and communities that are hurting cannot be motivated to engage in development dialogues while disregarding their hurt and trauma – these need to be part of the conversations too.

This chapter has opened up discussions on how best to use theatre for bringing people together to discuss their pain and the possibilities of forgiveness. But it is not limited to theatre; it could be painting, drawing, music, puppetry, videography, and the like. The key issue is to empower people to bring out their pain, confront it as part of designing and implementing their development interventions. In a community where women are constantly being sexually assaulted, injured or killed when walking alone, practitioners cannot talk about mobilizing people to contribute towards building a local school or health centre until the issue of security for women has been addressed – and to address this, requires that a communicative space be made available where women and those sexually assaulted can deal with this pain.

On the other hand, the chapter has dealt with the quintessential question of forgiveness. It has emphasized that crimes against humanity cannot and should never be forgiven. Yet, learning about the giving and asking of forgiveness allows for students to appreciate that in a world where there seems to be an obsession with justice and retribution, in which we all appear angry or dissatisfied about one thing or another, there exists a separate pathway towards resolving conflicts. Theatre and art workshops allow people to explore pain and trauma and how best they can move forward.

The discussion emphasizes that community theatre, in its various forms, provides open spaces for people to interrogate their struggle with forgiveness instead of bottling up all this anguish. The example by John Kani as well as examples from places that have experienced similar challenges show that development practitioners are organic intellectuals. Because of this, they cannot come into a community and focus on development as if the context of pain is non-existent. It has to be acknowledged, it has to be brought out, so that it can shape the development process. This chapter however does not suggest that development practitioners should emphasize one way of forgiving. For some, forgiveness is a reality if it is accompanied by the pursuit of truth and justice. Hence it is conditional, from Derrida's perspective. For others, forgiveness is a must; a moral, ethical, ideological, and political imperative – there is no escaping it. Its action is not conditional on any a priori set of factors; it is given notwithstanding. These are all possibilities that teachers of critical pedagogy should open up for development practitioners.

What is critical in these discussions – and this is the point the chapter is advancing – is that forgiveness is a world view; a perspective that could build individuals, communities, and societies. The world today, as noted in the foregoing, is or appears to be an angry place. Institutions of governance and accountability seem to be falling short of public expectations. It is possible to forgive and confront wrongdoing at the same time – the two are not mutually exclusive. To resist confronting evil means that we can refuse to address evil publicly and within official channels of communication, and yet confront it privately.

Note

1. The ruling party of Mozambique, known as the Liberation Front of Mozambique, or in Portuguese as *Frente de Libertação de Moçambique*.

CHAPTER 6
On leadership

After years of practice, I have come to appreciate that leadership and design are the underlying features of development practice. And they are not exclusive. In fact, I consider design to be a process through which a development practitioner exercises leadership. This chapter does not seek to contend with the various leadership thinking (systems versus analytical), but I do wish to focus on this notion of adaptive leadership. Nick Obolensky (2016) argues that there is a difference between systems and analytical thinking, in that the former looks at the meta-picture as a way to understand the small components, whereas analytical thinking examines the small units as a way of understanding the whole. This chapter will not debate what adaptive leadership is all about. It seeks to celebrate the Bantu notion of *utsogoleri* (leadership), which entails standing in the front but somehow leading from the back.

What this chapter seeks to explore, therefore, is how adaptive leadership can inspire development practitioners of the field to bring together stake-holders and communities in *co-designing* development that benefits the majority. For most development practitioners, our work largely involves, rather ideally, the co-creation of development solutions; that is designing development becomes a collaborative process of iterating and creating development interventions which address the genuine concerns of local people. To design is to create, to bring into being. Perhaps it is important to remember the immortal words at the time of creating the earth: 'let there be light'. This brought into existence not just the concept of time, but also laws of nature by which the sun becomes the centre of the solar system, and all planets revolve around it. In this case, therefore, design is not just the act of bringing things and the laws that will govern their operations into being, but it is rather a way of thinking. There is an inherent idea of the flow of power here; that implicit in creation is this sense of order and flow of laws and things.

Building on this classic example, we see that development has grappled with the question of design in certain ways. In the modernization paradigm, the main emphasis has been on the role of experts in thinking about, deciding upon, and settling on the kind of development people need. This brings in the theory of leadership as advanced by Socrates in Plato's *Republic*. Socrates (Plato, 2004) compares leadership to a ship captaincy. In a conversation with Adeimantus, Socrates discusses a ship owner who has very strong physical attributes but cannot see nor hear very well and has 'deficient' knowledge of 'seafaring'. As a consequence, the undisciplined sailors fight over who should be captain even when they have no skills. Yet the captaincy of this ship requires, for Socrates, 'a true captain must pay attention to the seasons of the year, the sky, the stars, the winds, and all that pertains to his craft if he is really going to be expert at ruling a ship' (Plato, 2004: 182). Which means in the modernist approach to development, it is the proverbial philosopher kings, or ship captains, who must decide what development is relevant for addressing the socio-economic needs of a community, country or region.

In this case, leadership is a responsibility of philosopher-kings, those with knowledge, resources, and education as well. For Marx and Hegel, however, the idea is that men and women are responsible for creating their own history. And while acknowledging that it is 'essential to destroy the widespread prejudice that philosophy is a strange and difficult thing just because it is the specific intellectual activity of a particular category of specialists or of professional and systematic philosophers', Gramsci (1932: 624) nevertheless contends that 'all men are philosophers'. This has a huge implication for the way we think about development. In fact, participatory development paradigms now emphasize the involvement of men and women in authoring development interventions. Leadership is not something local people expect of their development practitioners, as Socrates envisages: 'What is truly natural is for the sick person, rich or poor, to go to doctors' doors, and for anyone who needs to be ruled to go to the doors of the one who can rule him' (Plato, 2004: 182). Rather, leadership evolves from the interactions of the people and the development practitioners. In many cases, the leadership of the development practitioner entails identifying or working with a better local leader. In this way, development leadership entails facilitating and celebrating local leadership.

Utsogoleri and development leadership

Perhaps one question one has to ask now is: what does leadership in and for development look like? Is it about the work in the policy making sessions, where men and women in expensive clothes decide on what interventions are best suited for a demographic group or community? Is leadership about the high-level decision-making processes? I have seen graduate programmes in leadership being introduced for and with 'rising' or 'upcoming' leadership from the global South, so that they can meet the growing 'leadership needs' of growing economies. But is it true that we can train to be leaders in that way? What about the common people, like my mother or grandmother? Does it mean that their work and life can never be categorized as leadership?

To start this conversation, it is imperative that I make it clear that leadership (*utsogoleri*) and management (*kulamulira*) are two different things. In many cases, we see managers – highly autocratic, abusive, condescending, sexist – who think micro-management is leadership. In some of the professional environments, they write long emails, are extremely rude, cannot communicate well in person, and cannot communicate even with their teams – perhaps hoping for the divide and rule tactics where they can bully individual staff into certain submission. These are merely managers, not leaders.

In Chichewa *utsogoleri* is all about leadership and implies common recognition about the ability of a respected person to provide guidance on any given issue. This recognition comes from long-term trust that a person has established within a given social context. To be considered *mtsogoleri*, one does not apply for any specific position – it is a situation in which one is only considered a leader. Consideration is important, because it entails that even if a person is not willing or refuses to identify themselves as a leader, the social-economic conditions people live under compel them to consider that person a *mtsogoleri*. To be a *mtsogoleri* entails acceptance by both peers and the culture in which one finds oneself. Being a *mtsogoleri* is the opposite of *bwana*, the boss.

In fact, *bwana* has authority or power delegated to them by holding a certain position in society. In other ways, to be a *bwana*, one has to have a delegated authority, *mphamvu*, which translates as power. *Bwana* has access to resources. *Bwana* can do and often does do what they want. *Bwana* can be imperial and abusive of their authority, and people cannot do anything about it. Because *bwana* is like God. A politician in the southern context is a *bwana*, so too a police officer, a teacher, a nurse, doctor, and the like ... these are positions that give the performers absolute power over life and death. A kind of necropolitical force. In a way, *bwana* who has been granted power has *ulamuliro* (the power to lead) – as opposed to *utsogoleri*, where one is accepted as a leader.

These concepts are not mutually exclusive; there are instances when one with *ulamuliro* transforms into *utsogoleri*. An agriculture extension officer who has been employed to provide science-based advice to local farmers (they have been provided with *mphamvu* – power) will, over the years of working with local farmers, build trust to the extent that they are perceived as *mtsogoleri* (leader). This is largely because of the way they relate to local people, but also because they are using their extensive knowledge and experience to build the local community.

This chapter advances the latter notion of *utsogoleri* leadership as a vehicle for genuine development efforts on the ground. Where *ulamuliro* is about observing management traditions, rules, and best practices, *utsogoleri* is about flexibility, about the ability to be adaptable (*kulolera*), hence, adaptive leadership. Adaptive leadership is about depending on other people, having faith in their ability to contribute knowledge and resources, and to share a commitment to show faith in the key performance indicators. It is about working with other people to achieve the desired objectives. In fact, Obolensky (2016: 136) imagines a leader-manager who has the big picture vision and charisma but may lack the micro-details of 'day to day things getting things done'.

What it means for development practice is that, for development practitioners, there is a clear difference between leadership and management, even if these are not entirely exclusive terms. Yet the differences are stark, and, as highlighted by Obolensky, leadership is more strategic, long term, empowering, inspirational, and with focus on the big picture; whereas management is more tactical, short term, and uses control and micro-management. Perhaps as a compromise between these two approaches, the notion of transformational leadership has been propounded to describe a consultative process through which leaders and their teams collaboratively build each other's motivation, aspirations, and values as a means towards achieving strategic goals (Obolensky, 2016).

What this means for development is that leadership in development practice is no longer a debate between leadership and management. Granted that within the participatory development paradigm, men and women are being challenged to own the process of development – therefore great development practitioners embrace co-leadership and co-management with people on the ground. After all, Gramsci argues, all men are philosophers, thence, they have the capacity for rationality to think, design, and plot a future that addresses their needs and goals. Therefore, in this case, just like Gramsci's observation, there is no special category of development practitioners of the field that would consider themselves exclusively as leaders. Because leadership is not a 'thing'.

Leadership is not something one does at a particular point in time. No one can put a finger on this thing, as it were, called leadership. In fact, leadership happens and manifests through other actions. It is only during the process of designing development that leadership comes into operation.

Designing development

Social science literature conceives design as both a theory and practice that largely involves participatory inquiry, reflection, collective remembering, and to a large extent, storytelling (Abdullah, 2018). For me the idea of designing is multi-faceted. From a Marxist perspective, design entails a collaborative experience, allowing us (leaders and the led) to co-design interventions that will transform and situate ourselves. To name is to label, says Freire, Gutiérrez, and, of course, Marx. In this case, designing as a creative process occurs in a communication context. The recognition for liberation theologians has been that God has endowed humans with the divine responsibility to 'possess and master the world' (The Second Vatican Council (1971). In this endeavour, people have the responsibility to 'cooperate' and 'share' knowledge, technology and resources in order to 'unify their creative work' (The Second Vatican Council, 1971). The performance and experience of design within our social context entails mimicking the work of the creator, God. It entails that we become co-creators with God, the original creator, *Muumbi* (Creator or Potter).

In this case, therefore, design can be considered a form of cooperative creativity, to borrow the words of *Communio et Progressio*. In these processes, experts and local people 'act as co-investigators' – and it is this involving local people in research that 'deepens their critical awareness' about a particular reality (Freire, 1970: 106). The question of critical awareness or conscientization looms large in co-design and co-creation approaches. Thompson notes in *The Making of the English Working Class*, that class consciousness was a product of the working-class ability to conduct their own investigations, educate themselves to read the word and the world. It is clear therefore that designing development entails three critical aspects.

The first aspect concerns recognition of the power of the people. Freire (1970: 90) equates dialogue to humility, noting that 'dialogue cannot exist without humility', and that 'the naming of the world, through which people constantly re-create that world, cannot be an act of arrogance'. After all, 'dialogue, as the encounter of those addressed to the common task of learning and acting, is broken if the parties lack humility'. To name, therefore, demands that one has acquired the relevant consciousness about a particular people and their development challenges and opportunities. To acquire this necessary consciousness, time and resources are invested in building sustainable and long-lasting relationships with the people acquiring that necessary class consciousness. In the legendary speech, 'The Ballot or the Bullet', Malcolm X (1964) discusses a particular brand of development cultivated around the notion of black nationalism. For Malcolm, the gospel of black nationalism entails that black people should exert control over their own: 'the politics of your community, the economy of your community, and all of the society in which you live in should be under your control' (Malcolm X,1964). In this case, black nationalism can be said to be an example of an attempt to name the world.

The second aspect of designing concerns transformation, which not only allows us to design things better, but also empowers us and our co-workers to situate ourselves better. We express our aspirations in design because such development design is very much predictive and aspirational. This aspect addresses one of the serious practical challenges facing development practitioners working in and on interventions that are poorly thought-out – often as a result of politicians trying to be seen to be doing something, especially on politically sensitive issues that compel them to act or to be seen to act on them. This has consequences for development practitioners especially in regard to their relationships with local groups. The question is: do they tell the people that they do not agree with the official approach and intervention, or do they keep quiet? This chapter offers some nuanced understanding of the concept of politicized development – one which might be politically expedient, but practically problematic.

The third aspect of designing development with the people concerns the opportunity to reject 'bullshit' development approaches. In *The Importance of What We Care About*, Harry Frankfurt (1988) introduces the theory of bullshit, explaining the concept as an alternative to the truth, in which public figures tend to talk about things that they have little or no knowledge of: 'The advertiser wants to gain sales, and the politician wants to gain votes' (YouTube, 2016). In this case usually they 'do not have anything valid to say, so they say whatever will interest the audience' (YouTube, 2016). He notes the fact that usually the 'vast and amorphous' term has been 'employed loosely as a generic term of abuse' (Frankfurt, 1988). Frankfurt distinguishes the bullshitter from the liar, noting that to lie requires knowing the truth, while 'producing bullshit requires no such conviction. A person who lies is thereby responding to the truth, and he is to that extent respectful of it' (Frankfurt, 1988: 131). In defining bullshit, Frankfurt (1988) argues that often bullshit occurs when a public official feels pressured to speak about issues that they have little knowledge on.

Within the theory and practice of development, bullshit would refer to deceptive representation, in which policy makers who have no understanding of particular development realities propose and implement interventions that are deceptive or 'pretentious'. These interventions have no bearing on the real-life situation on the ground, and in a way, demonstrate that they do not care that what they are doing is going to destroy people's lives – not because they are bad people, not because they don't understand the truth. But the truth for them does not matter at all. The main thrust of the paper comes from the 2007 John Howard Government's implementation of the Northern Territory Emergency Response (Higgins and Brennan, 2017). Responding to the official and media reports alleging increased cases of child abuse in Indigenous communities, the Emergency Response involved deployment of security personnel, welfare restrictions, widespread alcohol bans, and forced land leases. This discussion builds on the debate in our polity, regarding the rationale and ethics of that Intervention, and the representation issues that shaped the communication context leading to the Intervention.

The Northern Territory Emergency Intervention

As briefly mentioned in Chapter 1, on 21 June 2006, the Australian Broadcasting Corporation (ABC) programme *Lateline* featured a segment, 'Sex Slavery Reported In Indigenous Communities'. This report was preceded by a series of sensational clips and interviews with 'experts' that revealed cases of sexual abuse in Indigenous communities in the Northern Territory. Following this, the *Lateline* team, led by journalist Tony Jones, intensified the sensational reports, as observed by *National Indigenous Times* journalist, Chris Graham (2017):

> *Night after night, Tony Jones and his team revisited the issue, filing 17 stories in just eight nights. As they did, the media frenzy around sexual violence in Aboriginal communities grew. ... Six weeks into the frenzy, on June 21, Lateline dropped perhaps the most shocking revelations*

of them all. The story ... alleged that young Aboriginal children were being held against their will in Central Australia, and traded between communities as sex slaves. Some of the children were given petrol to sniff, in exchange for sex with senior Aboriginal men. The story centred on the community of Mutitjulu, a tiny town of around 400 situated, literally, in the shadow of Uluru.

The repercussions of this broadcast were severe as has been noted above. It was, as development experts emphasize, made clear that marginalized people can only develop themselves. The writers might argue the report was objective and did not call for the Emergency Intervention. Yet evidence shows that the report is somewhat problematic in three ways. The first problem revolves around its emphasis that the recommendations be implemented as a matter of urgency: 'It is necessary that this process of recovery begin now', observes the foreword, urging, 'we make a special plea for prompt consideration and acceptance of the principal tenets of the report as a matter of extreme urgency' (NT Government, 2007: 5–6). The leadership to execute these urgent recommendations was placed totally at the doorstep of the Northern Territory Government.

The second problem can be found in the 'Overview', which opens with an orientalist, archetypal description of an Aboriginal person, who is located in a binary opposition to a civilized western individual, without any reference to how colonialism and problematic policies have contributed to a breakdown and disintegration of this person and their Indigenous communities (NT Government, 2007:5–6). It is very difficult to see how any Aboriginal person would be seen outside the lens of drunkenness, criminality, and primitivism – the very attributes that modernist development seeks to civilize.

Third, the report ignores other reports into the same problems carried out by reputable Indigenous organizations and scholars. It ignored several other expert reports from Aboriginal groups, scholars (such as Professors Judy Atkinson and Boni Robertson) and organizations (such as Top End Women's Legal Service, and the defunct Aboriginal and Torres Strait Islander Commission, ATSIC). One major criticism points to *Lateline*'s featuring a white Australian, Gregory Andrews, an Assistant Secretary in the Office of Indigenous Policy Coordination, as an 'Anonymous Youth Worker' (NITV, 2017). The programme thus allowed this serious misrepresentation, made worse, considering this person had not lived in the communities. Again, Marx's observation comes into play, the orientalist assumption being that Indigenous groups are incapable of representing themselves. Indigenous communities, organizations, and institutions have since disputed most claims in the programme.

As the Emergency Intervention was being announced by Prime Minister John Howard in Canberra, even Clare Martin, the then Chief Minister of the Northern Territory, claimed she was not aware of what was coming. The Intervention comprised extra police presence, health workers, stringent land leases, restrictions on welfare payments, and the like. It seemed, as observed by Miriam-Rose Baumann, a Nauiyu community resident, 'that they were going to take the community with them in trying to sort out what was needed in the community'. Likewise, Dorothea Randall, a Mutitjulu resident observed, 'it was unnecessary to have this intervention'.

So how do these developments feature in the meta-discourses of communication and development? Speaking at the opening of the International Communication Association Conference, Sonia Livingstone (2008) contended, 'spheres and their intersections have become mediated', later adding, 'everything is mediated'. What did she mean and why would that be important in this discussion of the implication of media reporting in government and institutional intervention in marginalized communities? The next sections examine the question of communication intervention in relation to concepts of orientalism and representation. Thus, it is important for the development practitioner to build trust and show local people that you are on their side.

As in all modernist development, the Emergency Intervention involved, from the Federal Government perspective, a financial investment package for delivering programmes in new housing, health, and education. As if agreeing with local residents, the Minister for Indigenous Affairs, Nigel Scullion, suggested, 'it would have been far better to do some of the same things with the full compliance of the community, rather than the community having the sense that it was imposed on us' (ABC News, 2017). Despite the politics largely influencing this unnecessary intervention, how do we explain the inability of experts and governments to listen to evidence? Why do we seem to ignore evidence or refuse to listen to it, but instead choose to listen to our stereotypes and orientalist fantasies? Perhaps this problem is partially rooted in our degree programmes. Thousands of degree programmes offer students an opportunity to read books endlessly, without paying attention to developing their skills and tools in listening. Indigenous cultures, on the other hand, have well-developed systems for storytelling and listening.

Similar interventions have been implemented the world over. In much of Africa, politicians have attempted to win over development practitioners of the field. The subsidy programme in Africa has involved the government providing cheap fertilizer to subsistence farmers, with the objective of ensuring food security at the local level. Yet the delivery of these interventions has often prioritized certain powerful individuals in the community, therefore to an extent, the people who most need these interventions are often left behind, largely because they belong to wrong political entities; or worse still, the delivery and distribution is fractured along ideological lines. In this case, therefore, fertilizer subsidies for subsistence farmers are huge vote winners even when after harvest, peasant families have no food, and the government has to buy and subsidize and distribute relief food items.

Development practitioners of the field are usually government employees. As civil servants, they are usually paid very late; they are poorly paid – and even if their contributions are critical towards ensuring government policies are implemented on the ground, they lack job security. With an influx of development organizations, their survival has often depended on allowances provided towards their support of NGO interventions that are often short term, short-sighted, and which rarely build on previous efforts or efforts of other implementing partners. And sometimes, development practitioners find themselves in conflict or competition with other development practitioners – when they work for development organizations. These organizations engage in an undeclared competition against each other or against the government departments responsible for a specific intervention. Perhaps as a way of demonstrating they are better equipped to understand and resolve local development challenges. As such, development capacity is constantly being contested and negotiated by competing political interests, and it is at the nexus of this ideological contestation that the development practitioners of both the office and the field find themselves.

This chapter/book does not intend to provide a step-by-step guide on how best to avoid such a pitfall – because there is no way to avoid it. This brings us to the unwritten contract a development practitioner has with the people: that we are there to represent their interests.

Elsewhere, Marx writes, 'They are therefore incapable of asserting their class interest in their own name, whether through a parliament or a convention. They cannot represent themselves; they must be represented. Their representative must at the same time appear as their master, as an authority over them, an unlimited governmental power which ... sends them rain and sunshine from above (Marx, 1852/2010). What Marx describes here is a situation in which marginalized groups are disempowered by hostile socio-political interests. These are groups that are left behind by twisted political and economic interests who benefit from people's voicelessness and powerlessness.

The contract with the people

The question would ideally be, why are we there in the community? Why do we want to work with and for the people? The idea of institutions sharing control with the people is classic in its origins. It is about giving power to the people. It is about giving people the leverage to negotiate their own destiny through elected representatives, and in cases where that does not work, publicly advocate for that change.

The idea of contract with the people emerges from modern governance theory – where it is assumed that governance is all about the people. The Progressive Party (1912) presented a 'Contract with the People' in which it professed: 'we hold with Thomas Jefferson and Abraham Lincoln that the people are the masters of their constitution', that this country belongs to the people 'who inhabit it'. And that 'to fulfil its purposes and to safeguard it from those', 'old parties', in which to deconstruct this 'invisible government, to dissolve this unholy alliance between corrupt politics and corrupt politics is the first task of the statesmanship of the day' (The Progressive Party, 1912).

The thoughts shaping these debates come from classic philosophers such as John Locke and Jean-Jacques Rousseau whose ideas on social contract have formulated the backbone of modern governance theory. This centres on the sanctity of the people's right to govern themselves. 'Being there' in the community entails working together with people in their ideological and empirical struggles against oppression and structures of inequality.

Extensive development literature discusses numerous tools and strategies that development practitioners can draw upon in order to build deep relationships with local people. One of the strongest arguments about development is that many development practitioners live off site, visiting the communities on a regular basis. The idea of development practice is concerned with mastering local life, and as such, even if the development practitioners of the office can live outside communities, the field practitioners should live there. Or in similar contexts. How does one understand the stress of drawing water from the river while enjoying the luxury of running water?

Being there in the community – the visibility, the reality of 'being there' – is the first article in the Contract with the People: this idea of sitting down with people in the sand, exchanging greetings, attending funerals and celebrations. The act of being there is the validity of that contract.

Power analysis

One of the instruments of mastering local socio-economic terrains involves studying how power flows in the local contexts, because it allows the practitioner to establish a working relationship with the community. Meetings with government and local NGOs bring in ways of challenging the problematic policies that are advocated and pushed by external interests. Yet there are a number of strategies for studying local power flows; first, it is important to conduct a community audit with the people: How much do we know about our community? What resources do we have? What do we want? How do we get where we want to be? What attributes do we need in our external partners?

Many community development centres and research initiatives have proffered numerous methods and strategies for conducting community audits within which power analysis looms large. The work of Robert Chambers (1981, 1994) in participatory rural appraisal (PRA) and participatory action research shows the critical significance of bringing the people into the development research process. Chambers conceived PRA as, 'a growing family of approaches and methods to enable local people to share, enhance and analyse their knowledge of life and conditions, to plan and to act. PRA has sources in activist participatory research, agroecosystem analysis, applied anthropology, field research on farming systems, and rapid rural appraisal (RRA)' (Chambers, 1994).

Designing as an encounter with God

At this point I would like to pay attention to a salient feature of my pedagogy, research, and practice – and that is God. I do understand that often within the academy, perhaps apart from theology or similar departments, the idea of discussing God seems opaque, uncivilized, unprogressive, mediocre. One of the key features of our public cultures today is the emergence of an advocacy that looks at people as a category of distinct races, tribes, or any kind of social grouping that seems significant at that particular point in time. Perhaps a point of departure is Kanye West, who, while acknowledging that we deal with various forms of social discrimination, discusses how we focus on the 'micro of it, and that we focus on the different races, as opposed to the macro, which is the human race' (Digital Madheads, 2015). Like West's notion of the human race, where 'our power, our oil, is our expression' (Digital Madheads, 2015). In the same vein, in *Fratelli Tutti*, Pope Francis discusses the notion of common brotherhood (Vatican Council, 2020). This is a discourse in which there is a kind of 'fraternal openness that allows us to acknowledge, appreciate and love each person, regardless of physical proximity, regardless of where he or she was born or lives' (Vatican Council, 2020).

Pope Francis discusses the questions of 'fraternity and social friendship', which allows us to experience an 'openness of heart', beyond social trajectories of nationality, colour or religion. For the Pope, our responsibility as human beings is to acknowledge the 'dignity of each human person, we can contribute to the rebirth of a universal aspiration to fraternity' (Vatican Council, 2020). In this form of social brotherhood or sisterhood, any sort of disagreement is frowned upon, and if there are any debates, they 'degenerate into a permanent state of disagreement and confrontation' (Vatican Council, 2020: Section 15). On the other hand, there is a possibility of the need to 'think of ourselves more and more as a single-family dwelling in a common home' (Vatican Council, 2020: 17). This leads us to ask one fundamental question.

Fratelli Tutti, a new theory of development practice?

One of the questions I have grappled with in development theory and practice is: what is the real theory of development practice? Especially where it concerns people doing development in the community. Is it theatre for development? Communication for development? Social and behavioural change communications? Or social psychology? Participatory action research? Or community engagement? What should ideally go into development field practice, theoretically speaking?

Fratelli Tutti opens up this theoretical framework by highlighting five key building blocks of this new development practice theory that entails celebrating Kanye's 'human race'. First, the Holy See advances the idea of a 'fraternity and social friendship' in which no one is superior to the other, thus emphasizing that we are all equal, and, just like St Francis of Assisi, emphasizing an 'openness of heart, which knew no bounds and transcended differences of origin, nationality, colour or religion' (Vatican Council, 2020). What this demonstrates is that our equality is natural, cannot be negotiated, and should not be, which means that entering into a people's contract is based on this recognition: that we are all brothers and sisters. This has a huge implication for development practice, as it entails that no one is superior at diagnosing the development challenges people face.

Second, a new development practice theory compels us to celebrate new forms of integration. In *Fratelli Tutti* (chapter 1, paragraphs 10 and 11) there is a recognition that for much of the western world, 'there was the dream of a united Europe, capable of acknowledging its shared roots and rejoicing in its rich diversity'. But this dream is being met with 'certain aggression' in which 'Ancient conflicts thought long buried are breaking out anew, while instances of a myopic, extremist, resentful and aggressive nationalism are on the rise' (Vatican Council, 2020). What the Encyclical is advising, therefore, is a renewed vocational practice, where we are involved in not just celebrating diversity, but also knowing each other and finding each other. After all, we are all neighbours. In fact, this *Fratelli Tutti* discusses the sermon regarding the Good Samaritan, in Luke 10, in which Jesus demonstrates through story-telling how a Jewish man, assaulted and hurt in a robbery, is abandoned by his tribesmen only to be rescued and recovered by a Samaritan – an ethnicity considered antagonistic by the Jews. This story teaches us that neighbours do not necessarily live next to us, but that, 'When our hearts do this, they are capable of identifying with others without worrying about where they were born or come from.' In the process, we come to experience others as our 'own flesh' (Vatican Council, 2020). This suggests that all forms of oppression are not welcome in this new humanism – and that includes slavery in all its forms, as well as 'varieties of narrow and violent nationalism, xenophobia and contempt, and even the mistreatment of those who are different' (Vatican Council, 2020).

Third, is the centrality of dialogue. In chapter 6, the Holy See discusses the need for 'Approaching, speaking, listening, looking at, coming to know and understand one another, and to find common ground: all these things are summed up in the one word "dialogue"' (Vatican Council, 2020). This means speaking to people or parties we do not agree with. The Encyclical observes that there is a tendency to 'choose the people with whom we wish to share our world', in ways that 'Persons or situations we find unpleasant or disagreeable are simply deleted in today's virtual networks; a virtual circle is then created, isolating us from the real world in which we are living' (Vatican Council, 2020: Para 47). Dialogue is a theme that has been emphasized in both liberation theology and Marxism. There is this idea that human beings, no matter their social standing, have an amazing ability to sit down and engage in conversations that will improve their lives. As discussed elsewhere in Freire, and in this treatise, dialogue is not just a communication process that defies the original theoretical frameworks in which there is only one communicator – in the *Fratelli Tutti* and liberation theology, dialogue can be confrontational yet loving, kind, and tolerant.

Fourth, the Encyclical discusses the need for wisdom. Wisdom comprises two aspects: First it is this 'faith experience' which is actually 'wisdom accumulated over centuries, but also from lessons learned from our many weaknesses and failures, we, the believers of the different religions, know that our witness to God benefits our societies'. And, second, wisdom is our recognition for God, his benevolence and his relevance in our daily lives. But God does not just refer to ideas from the *Bible* or the *Quran*; rather the lessons from my ancestors including my grandmother and great-grandmother, which constitute much wisdom, as outlined later in this book. The Encyclical advises that real wisdom should confront reality – especially in a time where reality can be revisited – to the extent that we do not know whether history is fiction, or what actually happened.

Fifth is the existence of a common moral good, despite a constant 'mockery of ethics, goodness, faith and honesty' (Vatican Council, 2020: Para 112).We live in a world where the boundaries of morality and what is socially acceptable are no longer confined to and defined by orthodox institutions of moral authority. Under 'Promoting the Moral Good', *Fratelli Tutti* discusses this question as a quest,'seeking and pursuing the good of others and of the entire human family also implies helping individuals and societies to mature in the moral values that foster integral human development' (Vatican Council, 2020).

Afterthoughts

This chapter has sought to demonstrate that the task and process of describing development in practice is much more complex than some of us may have imagined. There are two notions that may not be mutually exclusive, but they are constantly contending against each other: leadership (*utsogoleri*) versus management (*ulamuliro*). Leadership is all about social and local acceptance, whereas management depends on the delegated authority that a specific position has been granted, and beyond that authority, a person becomes useless. A leader, on the other hand, becomes so socially acceptable and respected that, even after so much time without interacting with a group or community, they will be well received if they reappear to greet local people.

What this means for development practice is that we should never under-estimate the power of local people accepting a development field practitioner as a leader. This chapter is celebrating the building of long-term and sustainable relationships with local people, as the only pathway that provides a kind of insulation to development practitioners to be seen as local and trusted. In this way, the discussion determines that one does not need an official position to be a leader. What this means is that, where management (*ulamuliro*) is given or granted by positions or portfolios, which gives an officer some sort of power (*mphamvu*), leadership actually happens (*kuchitika*). After all, for Thompson (1963: 8), the working class did not rise like the sun at an appointed time; it was present at its own making. This means, to be a development leader, one has to motivate people to be present at their own making.

CHAPTER 7
Wisdom of water

Beloved students of society,

Please allow me to talk about my great-grandmother's notion of people-centred development, *Nzeru za Madzi* (Wisdom of Water).[1] Whilst I acknowledge that few western authors have explored something similar, my notion of Wisdom of Water is rooted in indigenous communications, framed within post-colonial critiques, and was expounded to me by both my great grandmother and grandmother.

I want to believe that we remain committed to the ideals and virtues of exhorting humanity, even as our society undergoes various kinds of vicissitudes. I find it appropriate to open this conversation with an observation by the wonderful Roger Silverstone (1999:135), that 'all of what we do, all of who we are, as subjects and actors in the social world, depends on our relationships to others: how we see them, know them, relate to them, care for or ignore them. Seeing them is crucial.' It is with humility that I feel privileged to share some of my thoughts regarding how students of society can participate in the syntax, discourse and praxis of a people's pedagogy, in which we attempt to co-design deliberative development with and alongside people. It does not matter whether we are sitting in an office designing policies, conducting participatory research, or living on the frontline of development architecture right there in the community. We are all development practitioners. The reality is that even after completing studies, no one becomes an expert. Far from it.

In fact, it is just the beginning of our organized thirst and search for more knowledge on people, places, and time. Over and above the knowledge we gain from various formal training programmes in development practice, we need *indigenous intelligence* to enable us to navigate the dangerous and slippery waters of deliberative development. Such indigenous intelligence will not be found in formal education, even if one has studied anthropology or related subjects. What it means is that a person has just graduated into a student of the human condition, a student of society and a student of time. After all, we remain resolute in our collective commitment towards a democratic and deliberative reconstruction of our sick world. How does this indigenous intelligence enable us to, in the words of Silverstone above, 'see them'?

In fact, this is what this love letter is all about.

This love letter aims to enrich a number of positions regarding the seeing of others. Firstly, it explains the pedagogy of inclusion, empathy, love, and listening by providing a background to the process of growing up in a rural community, where I was raised by three wise women: my mother, grandmother, and great-grandmother. This has had a profound impact on the way I have viewed, pondered, and dealt with the subjects of empowerment, engagement, and the 'other'. Secondly, this letter outlines the key lessons that I have experienced from years of teaching in both the global South and the global North. My training in participatory communication at the universities of Malawi and Natal introduced me to indigenous knowledge and intelligence, empowering me to cultivate my own epistemological voice when it comes to capacitating development practitioners. In the end, the letter spells out key lessons for development practitioners of the field as they rename and reimagine the world alongside people.

For the Italian social theorist Antonio Gramsci (1932), history seems to have 'deposited' within us an 'infinity of traces without leaving an inventory'. As development practitioners, our main responsibility is to bring people together so they can contribute to the construction of this inventory 'at the outset'. The idea of this 'outset' is critical, granted that in the Marxist and Hegelian conception of history, the working class has always been present 'at its own making' (Thompson, 1963). It is the idea of historical groups owning and controlling the process of deconstructing and constructing their world. This chapter and this book are both about celebrating the agency of development practitioners in their attempt to co-design deliberative development. It introduces the *wisdom of water*, as a form of indigenous knowledge and intelligence through which development practitioners of the field cultivate their practice.

Wisdom of water

I grew up in the most impoverished places on the Earth. We did not have enough to eat when we grew up; the grass-thatched houses were small, poorly lit, and often stank; we shared the cramped living spaces with chickens and goats. Rats infested these spaces, and I remember waking up some mornings to discover these rodents had been nibbling on our heels. Our communities were located in lands left over from what colonial tea and tobacco estate owners had taken for themselves. As a result, we did not always have enough land to farm and grow our food, despite our people working hard on the land. And yet in all these economic predicaments, I did not hear one person in the community who defined us as poor. We suffered, yes, but we never saw ourselves as victims. 'Poor people' was an identity that I would, years later, come across in exotic development literature. We looked forward to community festivals, the traditional dances at night, when the women and girls would seductively shake their waists full of beads. We enjoyed the community food festivals held to celebrate a variety of causes. Even if there was not enough to eat in the individual families, there was always enough food for communal sharing. In a similar vein, Cleofe Torres, in feedback on this chapter, remembers growing up under such conditions in rural Philippines.[2]

Chapter 1 discussed how Chambers argues that 'meeting poor people is not so simple'. What this means is that doing development is not just about strategy and tactics, but about practitioners' sensibilities and mentality as well. Freire observes that for someone working with people where cases of family violence are involved, it is not just the strategy of bringing up this issue that must be engaged, but also finding the right time and *tactic* to raise this issue so that people do not feel they are being spoken at. Freire's tactic largely involves drawing on a practitioner's understanding of local sensibilities, or what anthropologist Clifford Geertz described as a structure of signification.

In most of the knowledge translation, the key steps are synthesis, generation, application, and exchange. In these knowledge and management models, knowledge creation is seen as a largely linear process even if it has an inbuilt mechanism for feedback.

This chapter argues that with *wisdom of water*, development practitioners eventually cultivate lasting relationships that enable people to talk more freely. As such, what this chapter examines is not necessarily a question of methodological strategies for approaching people, or for working in different cultural contexts. It is about cultivating our development practitioners with the wisdom of the people on top of the formal training which eventually hands them degrees and diplomas. But what is this wisdom of water? For my grandmothers, and so too in many indigenous contexts, there is this idea that a person can have a formal education and yet not have the wisdom of water. This *wisdom of the water* refers to the education of the people, rooted in their own ways of defining the world. It is in their songs, music, dance – it is embedded in their way of looking, of smelling, of speaking, and, often, of non-speaking. This is not necessarily referring to the initiation ceremonies for boys or girls, because with those there is an established pattern, content, structure, and season in which they are organized, and critically, such informal education has its own orthodoxy.

By *wisdom of the water,* I am referring to a structure-less and unspoken kind of traditional architecture that considers the whole life spectrum as a learning continuum connecting people with their culture and country. Its content emerges from the playgrounds where kids play; it filters in the hunting sessions by the men, the corn pounding experiences by the women; it is rooted in the proverbs, idioms, and stories that are shared around fireplaces and during funerals. It is the renaissance that distinguishes outsiders from insiders. From the perspective of Geertz (1973), wisdom of water could be construed as the 'webs of significance' and 'structures of signification' through which humans observe and interpret their world (Geertz, 1973: 5,7). It has a powerful hold on the formulation of identities, especially in closely knit societies. It is an education that enables local people to see and hear things that are not there; to smell things that no other nose can detect – it is a *pedagogy of feeling.*

The notion of wisdom of water celebrates the river, any river in indigenous lands, as the source of life, and thus the beginning of time. There is no development without water. And the river is both a symbol and fact of this historical materialism. But at the same time, wisdom of water, as articulated in the Martuwarra First Law, entails a peaceful and harmonious coexistence between humans and nature. Just like the architecture of indigenous laws elsewhere, the First Law comprises the 'body of laws which have governed relations between and within First Nations and between the human and non-human since the beginning of time' (Martuwarra River of Life et al., 2020: 544). For example, the Martuwarra River looks after the population of 7,000 within its catchment, and in turn, the local people look after the catchment, in which 'customary fishing, hunting and harvesting contribute substantially to local food security, as well as to cultural and medicinal practices' (ibid.: 543). In this scenario, a catchment is:

> more than just a place ... It is made up of human and non-human beings formed by the same substance, by the same ancestors, who continue to live in land, water and the sky. Country is family, culture and identity. Country, and all it encompasses, is thus an active participant in the world. Traditional Owners view Country as alive, vibrant, all encompassing, and fully connected in a vast web of dynamic, interdependent relationships; relationships that are strong and resilient when they are kept intact and healthy by a philosophy of ethics, empathy and equity ... Country is made up of human and non-human relations that speak Language and follow First Law (Martuwarra River of Life et al., 2020: 544).

For my grandmother, this wisdom of water tends to demonstrate three main attributes. Water is happy, water is bitter, but water is also sweet. In her view these attributes are not about taste, but rather the water's personal character – and I find this kind of indigenous epistemology to be relevant to this discussion of development practitioners. Happy water comes in many facets: rainwater, river water, water from the well, water from the village borehole, water from the mountain spring. And yes, it is all water, but it is not the same water. It may be used for various chores and reasons because of its properties as water, but it is not the same water. Happy water has this godly attribute of creation; it is *Muumbi*, the creator of life.

This *Muumbi* is seen in the water villagers use in cooking their food, washing their bodies. It is water that is used to feed animals, to build houses. The power of this *Muumbi* is seen in people's fields during or after rains, when the crops are thriving in the field, the crickets are singing, and the birds are twittering. One can smell the sweetness of *Muumbi* in the soil. The women are singing and chanting as they walk from the riverbank with pails balanced on their plaited heads. Men are planting crops in the fields, and we all know these seeds will lie in the soil for a few days, some of them will be eaten by the wild birds, yet with the warmth of the wet soil of *Muumbi*, the seeds will sprout and give people hope of a decent yield that year.

Muumbi is also showing its force in indigenous architecture. In local building and construction, houses tend to rely on the power of water. There are houses with bricks, houses with stones, or houses built with kiln bricks, and then there are houses constructed using traditional methods. But all these are constructed with water, more specifically muddy paste. Among the different kinds of houses are houses that are round in nature, known as *namurukunuwa*. In constructing these dwellings, builders start with strong tree poles supported by a woven network of bamboo or reeds, which then are sealed with a soil paste made from water and clay. These traditional houses will then have a door made out of bamboo and grass for easier entry and exit. The roofing is grass thatched, which provides natural insulation from the unpredictable weather, especially the warm temperatures. The floors are treated with indigenous medicinal paste to prevent termites, and then usually with wet clay. In other cases, animal dung, straw, and small stones are used to smoothen or create earthen floors. *Muumbi* is about creating spaces for habitation.

Water also enables people to decorate these traditional houses with multi-coloured paste commonly comprising soft soil, clay, water, charcoal, and ash. Though there is nothing gender-specific about this activity, it is typically carried out by women and girls. Men handle the construction and women provide the final touches and decorations, so in the end both parties contribute to the construction of the home. In most communities, the location of the dwelling is decided by women, chiefly in compounds where there are a number of families. These aforementioned uses of water are what my grandmother termed as happy and peaceful water.

My grandmother also talked about angry water, water that takes an interest in the behaviour of human beings. There is a mythical serpent snake, *Napolo,* that spends much of its life sleeping under a mountain (Chimombo, 2000). It feeds on human souls and bodies that get lost in the mountains. This snake possesses spirits which wander through the mountains, offering free food to travellers with specific instructions to eat the food only until they are full, then leave the rest there. Anyone who ignores these arrangements finds themselves lost, and eventually becomes food for the mythical serpent snake beneath the mountain. The time always comes when *Napolo* grows big from feasting on human souls and decides to move to a bigger body of water, hence the devastating flash floods. This is the serpent changing homes, usually preferring to live in the open ocean with a massive body of water.

The reason for this change of scenery could be because *Nangumi*, the water god, lives in the darkest depths of these oceans. Whether *Nangumi* is more powerful than *Napolo*, I can't be sure – nor can I be sure whether *Napolo* may actually be *Nangumi*. This water god has a short temper which is marked by the violent waves of the oceans. Calming *Nangumi*'s temper requires the sacrifice of human souls. 'Sometimes *Nangumi* is so angry she creates a wall with water, blocking a ship from proceeding on its journey', my grandmother would emphasize. 'When this happens, children and women have to be thrown into the water to calm her temper, softening her heart to allow the ship through.' Looking back, I don't think my grandmother's point in this story is that children and women had to be sacrificed. I think her point is that even the relationships people have with the most powerful forces and institutions that shape their welfare can be negotiated. There is no need to be overwhelmed by the sheer size of inequality and underdevelopment. There is always a way out, and usually the solution is not going to be brought into the community, rather the people have to make choices and sacrifices in order to redefine and author a new future and destiny.

Then there is water that is sweet, and I have often wondered: how can an attribute be conceived as sweet? It has dawned on me that what these folk stories really discuss here is the symbiotic and reciprocal relationship between and among elements in development relationships. In the previous two scenarios, water is still able to be happy or angry regardless of the attitude of the people. Its attributes are not dependent on the reception or behaviour of the people – it just is. Water as *Muumbi* predates people, and it is both a creator and destroyer.

Sweet water is different. It is about the historical process of making. Similar to the way Thompson discusses working classes being present at *their own making*, sweetness is that historical process in which men and women make history. This water does not predate man's activities and behaviours – it is created through the symbolic, sensual interactions between men and women involved in the experience of procreation. *Muumbi* is now a kind of creation, and later on becomes a Creator.

Sweet water is the product of a process that respects the individual skills, knowledge, and capabilities of the participants in any human endeavour, development included. The sweetness of the water can only be experienced in action, and the experience only lasts as long as there is this frictional interaction in which both or all parties are willing participants who respect each other. Epistemologically speaking, the participants are inside and outside each other. One would think development practitioners need to understand all these three attributes of water. It is clear from my grandmother that water exercises its wisdom in all these attributes. The question of understanding requires an explanation here. In indigenous contexts, to understand means more than comprehending a phenomenon – it implies listening for deeper meaning or reality.

For someone to understand the three layers through which we encounter water, one needs to listen, to smell, to know, and to make sense of the different contexts in which we encounter this water. This is the essence of development work: that field practitioners should be able to scan someone's face and be able to tell whether they are concerned, confused or okay about a particular scenario. This skill of perception cannot be taught in training programmes. It is acquired over time.

An ideal development field practitioner understands the three forms of water and is able to read them in the relational encounters with communities. The fields of anthropology or rural sociology recommend long-term ethnographic research. For Clifford Geertz, successful collaboration with local communities depends on one's ability to construct what Gilbert Ryle terms 'thick description' of people's behaviours, attitudes, and practices. In this case, doing development effectively requires one to do anthropology. For Geertz (1973: 10), 'doing ethnography is like trying to read a manuscript – foreign, faded, full of ellipses, incoherencies, suspicious emendations, and tendentious commentaries, but written not in conventionalized graphs of sound but in transient examples of shaped behaviour' (Martuwarra River of Life et al., 2020). In this case, the *wisdom of water* becomes a semiotic facility for reading this foreign and faded manuscript of local development.

Doing development with communities therefore means celebrating the first laws of the land, which, in many cases, entail the recognition of the spiritual heritage that shapes the daily lives of community members. For example, among the Martuwarra Nations, 'first law recognizes the River as the Rainbow Serpent: a living ancestral being from source to sea' (Martuwarra River of Life et al., 2020: 541). In celebrating this heritage, there is a deliberate effort on the part of the development practitioners and communities to challenge the colonial conceptualization of development, which is all about enriching exogenous interests and capital. Co-creating development with people means writing a new development story and telling that story from the perspective of oppressed peoples – as a way to contest the meta-narrative of what Martuwarra River of Life et al. (2020: 542) and others conceive as 'non-consensual development'.

So, what are the key lessons I want to share with students of society regarding field practice in development? An apt anecdote comes from the village where I grew up. My grandmother had just prepared lunch and we were about to enjoy the meal which was still in the kitchen. Out of nowhere arrived a visitor. There was not enough food even for us, so we continued chatting without bringing out the food. Even the hungry children did not dare mention the word food for we knew that we were reserving it for ourselves only. Once the visitor left, we were able to bring out our lunch. What the *wisdom of water* refers to here is this intricate knowledge of inner workings of a society or community that is borne out of experience, enabling us to understand the underlying currents in human relationships.

No field manual will teach that. The field manual might discuss what kind of clothing is appropriate for visiting communities or the way we speak. Theatre for development or participatory research training sessions do build capacity in how to approach communities. Yet *wisdom of water* cannot be learnt in school. It is not something that one would learn in cultural sensitivity training. It is a deep-held attribute that compels us to see others as human beings, and from that vantage point, we are able to build and sustain quality human relationships. The argument here is that only a field practitioner who is imbued with people's wisdom, one who has fallen in love with people will be able to exercise empathy, forgiveness, love, listening, and gender and cultural sensitivity in their praxis.

Wisdom of water enables development practitioners, importantly, to exercise faith in people they work with. They are not going into communities to babysit people into development, as is fantasized in modernist interventionist models. Development field officers are there first and foremost to exercise faith that the people have the capacity and ability, with minimal support, to drag themselves out of the quagmire of inequality they are drowning in. As a consequence, the *wisdom of water* proffers a development practice that is rooted in collective experience. Yet the question remains: How can *wisdom of water* be taught to development practitioners of the field? I think the answer lies in storytelling.

Storytelling and the colour of words[3]

My development practice has been shaped by a number of scholars, rivers, seasons, and epistemologies. The meeting with Chris Kamlongera and Chijere Chirwa at the University of Malawi in the 1990s introduced me to the idea of doing history with people; Keyan Tomaselli at the University of Natal in early 2000 fundamentally challenged the way I thought about us–them relationships; the theatre for development experiences on donor-funded social mobilization projects upended my understanding of development, but also developed my love for storytelling. It cemented for me that each development intervention starts with and ends with a story. And my encounter with Mukhwiri Jonathan Makuwira, whose pedagogy of simplicity continues to influence the way I write, think, and express myself.

Perhaps it is for this reason that my scholarship, my pedagogy, and my practice are all fascinated by one fundamental question: How do we capture, make sense of, and utilize citizens' voices so that they inform dominant and orthodox policy development, formulation, implementation, and evaluation? Thus, the question is: Why do stories matter? Why should we be interested in examining, in contesting, and in looking at the role of storytelling when it comes to sustainable development? I want to take you back to 11 September 2001. In the aftermath of that tragedy, there were so many discourses within our public spheres and public media, demonstrating a palpable anger – perhaps most notably among certain groups of people regarding traditions and ways of looking at life. As a result of that anger, that discourse of outrage and disappointment, the media picked up and mobilized toxic narratives – narratives that pushed the western governments to go to war in Iraq and Afghanistan.

Now, those wars have not brought about any peace or development. In fact, they have brought more devastation. They have generated mistrust between civilizations. The most important aspect I wish to point out to you is the role of storytelling in what Mahmood Mamdani describes as the 'politics of naming' (Mamdani, 2007). What this entails is that the media and establishment punditry contribute to the creation of a discourse of intervention. They can call for military intervention today, and then, tomorrow, call for engagement and discussion as a way to resolve a conflict they created in the first place. I am not here to litigate the moral justification of military intervention – I am more interested in having a conversation about how stories can challenge or poison the way we look at the world. The question I would like us to answer is: What is the role of stories and narratives in cultivating *wisdom of water*, particularly, wisdom of water regarding complex cultures and ways of life that Lerner's western modernity erroneously claimed wanted to be westernized?

One of the ways in which stories can contribute to cultivating wisdom of water – which eventually promotes sustainable peace and cohesion – is through educating people about the richness and beauty of the lives of people who are different. In the revised introduction to the wonderful book, *Orientalism*, re-written after the 11 September attacks, Edward Said emphasizes the importance of learning about other cultures in order to enrich our understanding of how we interpret the world. By employing wisdom of water, journalists and storytellers promote stories that advance development and peace. Such wisdom helps us to celebrate people who are different; people who look different, walk differently, smell different, and who look at the world in ways we cannot first imagine. Wisdom of water therefore helps us understand the boundaries and redlines in a multicultural environment. For example, certain representations of religious symbols and figures should be avoided if they elicit fiery emotions in some people, even if laws permit us to do so. In other words, wisdom of water operates in the liminal spaces where law can spur conflict.

The second point concerns stories as vehicles for wisdom, enabling people to name and create a new world. There is a verse in Genesis where God says, 'Let there be light', and right there, the day was created. Stories give us that Godly character, of creation, of bringing dreams and imagination into life. Through stories, we bring to life certain ideas, values, beliefs through the characters that tell these stories. We give these stories what the writer-philosopher Hannah Arendt describes as 'the human condition', or what Raymond Williams describes as the 'structure of feeling'. Informed by the wisdom of the people, stories enable us to celebrate the voices and identities of people who are often left behind by modernity and globalization. That is the power of stories – they are imbued with the ability to define.

The third aspect I consider important is that narratives and storytelling are a window into wisdom of water, or people's wisdom. They allow us to feel and listen to what is going on around us. Narrative, and of course storytelling, enables us to travel into liminal spaces, constructing a world based on the lived experiences of the people we are writing about. People are then able to imagine themselves in these stories – to *see* themselves in the stories. In order to unpack the notion of speech, stories and narratives allow us to make a distinction between who is speaking and who is not.

The question is: How can we use storytelling to capacitate development practitioners of the people to master and understand the wisdom of the people?

The first strategy concerns building long-term relationships with people. I am not referring to transactional relationships motivated by extractive benefits – obtaining information, knowledge or resources – but rather long-term, symbiotically beneficial and sustainable relationships. For instance, even if there is no other reason, a person can make a phone call or pay a visit to ask how the children and the community are doing. Because when we talk about building long-term, sustainable relationships, they are meant to be mutually beneficial relationships. So, on one hand, we are kept informed about the goings on and we have to be genuinely interested. Remember people's names, names of places, ongoing challenges – and perhaps being able to link people to critical service providers. As such, there develops this kind of cultural transaction wherein we offer something back symbolically to their community.

Perhaps another strategy would be to learn about other cultures with the aim of enriching our own understanding. We ought to travel the globe. To learn a second language. These will be constant reminders of other worlds beyond ours. We need to learn things with different people, Freire advises – a contrasting cultural dance or performance. We need to talk to people. We ought to try to speak different languages. If we are visiting a particular community or living in a particular country, the least we can do is to practise talking to people in their own language. It feels good even if one's pronunciation may not be perfect, we can be sure that we are appreciating local cultures and local traditions. It helps us to appreciate the totality of the way people live their lives.

A further strategy is to reflect other people's ways of looking at the world. There is this notion of perspective or *Weltanschauung*. This refers to the way people look at things. Do our stories reflect the way people look at the world? James Baldwin challenges us to question our privileged way of viewing the world, which we have discovered through his notion of 'the view from here' (Baldwin, 1986). When we write history, tell a story, or construct a narrative, we may present a view from here rather than a view from there. Moving from a view from here to a view from there requires a number of things. It requires that our ways of looking at the world be educated and be cultivated by a particular understanding of the *wisdom of water*.

There is something magical about storytelling, as I recall growing up some time ago. Gathering as children around my grandmother and great-grandmother, we would listen to their stories. These stories captured our imaginations, not only because they were beautiful, but because there was a magic about the words. American writer Maya Angelou observes:

> *Words are things, I'm convinced. In the beginning was the Word.*
> *And the word was God, and the word was with God. Words are things.*
> *You must be careful, careful about calling people out of their names,*

using racial pejoratives and sexual pejoratives and all that ignorance.
Don't do that. Someday we'll be able to measure the power of words.
I think they are things. They get on the walls. They get in your wallpaper.
They get in your rugs, in your upholstery, and your clothes, and finally
into you (Oprah Winfrey Network, 2014).

Storytelling as a strategy for achieving wisdom of water has huge implications for development practitioners and educators. In *Letters to Cristina*, Freire discusses the problem of undemocratic supervisors who occupy the minds of their supervisees, denying them the space to think independently. The consequence is that supervisors end up with disciples and not critical, well-rounded human beings. There is a terrible disease in the academy, in which students are occupied by supervisors who have a problematic relationship with the concept of freedom. On one hand, one sees the social media accounts of these professors showing off their progressive side, if such a side exists. Their profiles are full of nonsense related to how much they celebrate freedom of expression, that freedom is a fundamental human right. Yet when they enter their tiny offices and classrooms, these professors terrorize the heck out of their students by dictating how research projects are thought about and written. In the end one sees professors writing their own dissertations through the work of these students. It reaches a point of telling students what to think, what questions to ask, what theories to draft into a study, and what to do if they want to find favour with us as teachers.

For both teachers and students of development practice, wisdom of water engenders the *liberatory practice of storytelling and listening*. There is an assumption that listening is an act, which involves keeping quiet when someone is speaking. Well, part of it, yes, but there is more to it. Writing to explain her decision to join the conservative Fox News Television, Democratic Party Strategist, Donna Brazile (2019) observes the need to 'first be able to hear what others are saying without the filter of bias and contempt'. She emphasizes treating those with 'differing views with civility and respect' so that together we can 'solve the myriad of problems our country must overcome'. What Brazile is underscoring here – and this is the lesson we could all draw from if we want to benefit from listening – is that we have to experience it without any preconceived 'bias and contempt', which prevents us from seeing and finding each other.

Central to storytelling is also writing, or the art of it.

And, I think to write implies and simultaneously requires that we take sides, to go to war against certain perspectives, memories, and certain forms of forgetting.To write also implies connecting with our other interests in painting, music, film, fashion, and art. I do not think that one can write and divorce one's writing from one's artistic interests; say, for example, *The Baptism of Christ* by Andrea del Verrocchio (1472) which would be perfected by the apprentice Leonardo da Vinci.

At the same time, I also realize that writing is an exercise in contradiction. It is possible to write a postcolonial critique of development while building on western or colonial authors. Because in writing, authors that we employ are just the colours of paint we use, and what I do with that paint depends on how I mix the paint, the shadows, colours, and perspectives that will sketch the canvas.

To write, for me, is to embark on this journey that an author must undertake in order to initially copy and sound like those we admire, say Billie Holiday in *God Bless the Child* or Louis Armstrong in *What a Wonderful World* or Luciano Pavarotti in *Nessun Dorma*. Yet over time, writing in storytelling will push me towards that abyss where I must now sound like myself. As such, to tell a story implies that writing must have a sound and a rhythm to it. Miles Davis (Davis and Troupe, 1989) articulated this thought when he observed that it took him such a long, long time to play and sound like himself. Storytelling helps all of us to achieve that difficult virtue.

Pedagogy of *seeing* in action

There is a dusty road that meanders reluctantly from the University of Malawi's main campus of Chancellor College down Chirunga Forest. The road then slithers its way through the mostly grass-thatched houses and disappears into the infinity and oblivion of unresolved, uncontested, and infinite poverty. These villages would become a significant intellectual platform that enabled the late Professor Chris Kamlongera to provide a different kind of education. When I joined Chancellor College, I enrolled into the arts programme to study history and theatre for development. It is the decision to study the latter that would lead me to an encounter with, mentorship under, and long-term collaboration with Chris, a giant in communication for development in his own right. He introduced me to theatre for development, Paulo Freire, Augusto Boal, William Shakespeare, Anton Chekhov, Leo Tolstoy, Ngũgĩ Wa Thiong'o, Mbongeni Ngema, Chinua Achebe, Zakes Mda, and many other fantastic writers. He also taught our classes the meaning, power, and praxis of workshopped theatre and collective performance.

Instead of sitting in class and teaching us theories and concepts as is expected of orthodox and banking education, Chris herded our whole class into the surrounding villages by foot. He divided us into small teams and requested we engage with villagers. We would go from house to house, talking to residents about local development issues. Chris discouraged any notetaking, instead, emphasizing that we join the villagers in whatever activity they were undertaking.

'You have to listen', was his mantra at the beginning of each field exercise. Upon returning to classrooms, we would analyse the issues and then come up with plays. On an agreed date with the village leadership, we would perform these plays, which would bring in local participation. If he were concerned with the direction of a particular scene, he would join the performances as a drunken character to ensure we delivered the right messages. As a teacher of critical pedagogy, he was right with us, not above us.

This was my entry into the world of capacitating development practi-tioners. For Chris, development practice was not just about the democracy of the communicative process and its transformative attributes, in which media technology are just tools (if required) to facilitate that engagement. It was principally about falling in love with the people. This is the epistemo-logical essence that Chris instilled in us at the performance forums, while seated at the village arena, singing and performing with local people. If at first, we were big-headed in imagining we were change agents, Chris always reminded us that our being educated rested in learning from the wisdom of the people, and mastering the art of analysing the world from the perspective of local people.

We the students were not aware we were part of a larger intellectual scheme of things. That we were contributing to the radical deconstruction of the dominant syntax in the social sciences. When the Post-Crash Economics Society was established at the University of Manchester around 2012, Chris had already introduced us to the power of incorporating non-western perspectives into education –more than a decade before. Genuine education for Chris lay in capturing the hopes and aspirations of local people, in celebrating the *wisdom of water*. It was about knowing and seeing other people, as Silverstone described in 1999.

Years later, Professor Kamlongera would leave the university to engage in communication for development practice. He, alongside other development experts, would generate rigorous research, testing new models and publishing great scholarship and policies in participatory development. He brought me on board when he tested some of the methodologies such as the partici-patory rural communication appraisal, during which we attempted to develop communication strategies with farmers, fishermen, and all kinds of local people.

In taking time off from teaching to undertake development practice, Chris showed that a progressive scholar should leave the classroom, learn the wisdom of the people, and also allow for the empirical testing of their ideals. Alongside these professional experiences, Chris also consulted for and advised governments and development organizations. He would return in mid-2000 to the same University with the aim of establishing Africa's first ever MA programme in communication for development – something that had never materialized due to the complexity of institutional politics.

After my undergraduate degree, I was offered a scholarship to study for the Master of Arts at the University of Natal. It was here that I met Keyan Tomaselli, who introduced me to public health communication and visual anthropology. It was he who would introduce our class to critical literature in representation, power, ethnography, semiotics, and indigenous knowledge. Even if the readings were heavy, both he and Ruth Tomaselli made it interesting and enjoyable to study Gramsci, Althusser, Stuart Hall, Thompson, Jay Ruby, Charles Sanders Peirce, Roland Barthes, Robert Flaherty, Timothy Asch, and so many others.

Yet it was our participation in the field projects that would be epistemo-logically liberating, opening our eyes to a critical pedagogy I had partially experienced before. The Centre for Communication, Cultural and Media Studies (CCMS) at Natal had established long-running collaborative research projects with civil society institutions and community groups. These were the *Semiotics of the Encounter* and *Rethinking Indigeneity* Projects. I joined the CCMS, and made two trips to Northern Cape, into Southern Kalahari. Field work with Tomaselli involved almost 'doing nothing', other than walking around the community and talking to people, joining them in whatever activities they were embarking on. Much of it was what one would define as 'participatory mapping'. Truth is, it never felt like we were *doing* research, more so chatting to people. Yet, research happened in the process of learning with the people.

Tomaselli, just like Kamlongera before him, never carried a notebook, a recording device, a bag, or anything. He was casual about his conversa-tions and his dealings. As a new MA student, I was not sure what I would be studying here, until late one morning, we came to a household where there were a number of women. It was during these unscripted and unrehearsed research exercises that I, alongside other student researchers, experienced the first photo elicitation session (Manyozo, 2017). Tomaselli was conversing with a local woman, Rosa Meintjies, focusing on a black and white copy of her family photograph, taken by Donald Bain for a 1936 photographic exhibition. There were also other modern shots of Meintjies' family standing side-by-side, given to the family by another researcher of indigenous communities. These photographs did not identify the subjects. In an informal manner, Tomaselli strategically shifted the conversation to the photographs, asking Meintjies to activate or provide realism operators to the pictures by assigning a context which is often missing in inactivated ethnographic photography.

I have reported that 'in a spontaneous moment of photo elicitation, Meintjies tearfully activated a long history of dispossession, of ancestor remembrance and genealogy by explaining the significance of the photographs, which to us, with preconceptions and ignorance, had, until that emotional moment, merely been inactive texts'. Her reading of the series of inactivated photographs indicated that active interpretation is a convergence. It is a convergence of photographs as cultural texts; the circuit of culture of the photographed, the circuit of culture of the photog-rapher, the circuit of culture of the reader, and the circuit of culture of the context in which the reading is taking place. It was this encounter that would motivate me to study the semiotics of indigenous photography. Over the months that followed, I embraced this kind of research, studying photographers working in the community and at the same time, observing how subject communities related to and with the photographers. It was the second time I had seen critical pedagogy integrating *wisdom of water*.

I have had the rare honour and privilege of knowing both Kamlongera and Tomaselli as teachers, friends, and colleagues. Yes, they have personified communication for development, but most importantly, they have shown that *pedagogy of seeing* can be a guiding philosophy that allows experts and people to collaboratively and democratically contest power in the formulation and implementation of effective policies. Over and above the invaluable knowledge they have generated as scholars, their greatest achievement was to be professors of the people: at the village universities located in the songs, in people's wisdom, in the sand, the music, and the food. I think they both showed that education means nothing if we have no skills nor wisdom to connect with people – that we should seek the relevance of knowledge in the lived realities of people.

Being the salt of the earth

At this juncture I want to turn our attention to a topic that many in the academic spaces rarely allude to: God. It is often assumed that all this discussion of development can be realized in a spiritual vacuum. That financial, technological, and technical resources can be harnessed by good people and guided by good planners, supported by good implementers which will enable good people to 'receive' development.

I want to explain that reference to God here is meant to emphasize my earlier arguments about the values development practitioners must have to be effective co-designers and implementers of sustainable development. The key argument laid out hitherto is that practitioners of the field must exercise humility, being able to listen to, care for, and love the people.

All these attributes are well articulated by Gustavo Gutiérrez's notion of preferential option for the poor. Thus, the idea that our development practice is in a way a kind of pastoral assignment that allows us to demonstrate our love for both man and God. In fact, Gutiérrez recognizes that even if we claim to be atheists, doing development with the people is itself an act of love for God.

In Matthew 5: 13, Jesus says to his disciples, 'You are the salt of the earth, but if the salt loses its saltiness ... it is no longer good for anything.' Then continues in verses 14 and 16, 'You are the light of the world ... let your light shine before others, that they may see your good deeds and glorify your father in Heaven.'

To do development with people requires that practitioners exercise spiritual qualities outlined in these Bible verses and perhaps in other similar spiritual texts such as the Quran. Being the 'salt of the earth' or the 'light of the world' entails practitioners standing out for their kindness, humility, approachability, and very much being genuinely interested in the welfare of the people.

In conclusion, this chapter settles three key determinations from this book.

The first is that development practitioners of the field should work towards establishing long-term relationships with others. These are not extractive interconnections but rather mutually beneficial interactions in which outsiders and insiders collaboratively co-design their world. The second is this idea of knowing other people. Said (1978) highlights the importance of studying other cultures with the aim of enriching our understanding of others. This is what 'knowing' others means, that the respectful associations we form with other people will enrich our understanding of them. The third critical aspect revolves around 'seeing them'. By 'seeing' them, Silverstone is referring to perspective, as a frame of reference that allows us to make sense of things. In this case, if we are trying to make sense of a people and a culture, we should make the effort to find them, to understand them from their perspective. If we are to twist Baldwin's observation, we would argue that in seeing others, we adopt the 'view from there'. It is these three aspects that make all of us students of society, students of the human condition.

Perhaps a memorable lesson that Kamlongera and Tomaselli have taught us is well captured by the Spanish poet, Antonio Machado, who seems to observe that the traveller is responsible for creating the road they should walk on (*Caminante, no hay camino, se hace camino al andar*). Both Tomaselli and Machado seem to be challenging all of us today to actively intervene in creating a society that is equal and democratic by walking this symbolic road. Both have travelled dusty trails into people's communities and homes, which opened intellectual and professional avenues for many of us. Over and above their many publications, Chris and Keyan have always respected and celebrated the wisdom and knowledge of local people.

Let us all, as students of time, students of the human condition, and students of society, resolve to walk these symbolic dusty, windy, and unforgiving roads in search of the pedagogy of listening, in which we celebrate the *wisdom of water*, not for the sake of it, but to enable us to employ the local 'structures of signification' to build more humane communities and societies. And where there are no roads, we will create new ones.

With so much love, imperfect it might be, today, forever, and always.

Linje Manyozo
Gippsland, Victoria
Australia

Notes

1. The story of *Nzeru za Madzi* (Wisdom of Water) was not told to me as a coherent whole, nor was it told in one encounter, not even to one person. It was very interrupted; and I have never considered it a story in singular – rather these were a series of interrupted stories – *Nzeru za Madzi* was a collective cultural experience, told to different family members at different times: Part of it was from my favourite person in the world, *Anganga*, my second grandmother *Lydia Chipojola*. The critical part of the story was last explained to me by my great grandmother, *the Agogo – Abiti Bisani* – when I last saw her in 2006, at the time I was

reading for my PhD – and I had come to say my farewell, knowing she was beyond a century, and her transitioning was nigh.

2.   In emailed comments to this manuscript, Cleofe Torres recalls that:

> It is good that you bring out that very truthful story about poor people not defining themselves as such. I got that same experience: I grew up in a small neighbourhood in a village where many families could be considered poor; no TV, house made of wood with 'silong' (cellar) where firewood, chickens and pigs are kept for immediate household needs. Everybody would eat almost the same local food. And we have learned to be content having our only pair of slippers replaced once a year during Christmas time. But nobody thought he was poor. Until I reached college, I met students from other areas in the country. And by the standard of what they wear and use in school, I realised I come from an economically deprived family.

3.   Part of this section was delivered as a pre-recorded keynote address 'Colour of words' for a University of Queensland Rotary International Class XVII Peace Fellow Seminar that was cancelled due to the global Covid-19 pandemic. Available: https://vimeo.com/431669570

References

Abdullah, D. (2018) A Manifesto of Change or Design Imperialism? A Look at the Purpose of the Social Design Practice; Bailey, J., Lloyd, P. (2016). 'A View from the Other Side: Perspectives on an Emergent Design Culture in Whitehall'. *Proceedings of ServDes 2016, the Service Design and Innovation Conference*. Copenhagen, Denmark, 24–26 May.

ABC News (2017) 'A look at how the Commonwealth Intervention into the Northern Territory has impacted communities 10 years on' [online] <https://www.abc.net.au/news/2017-06-21/how-commonwealth-intervention-in-nt-impacted-communities/8637298?nw=0> [accessed 30 May 2022].

Adichie, C. (2009) 'The danger of a single story', TED Talk, Oxford University [website] <https://www.youtube.com/watch?app=desktop&v=D9Ihs241zeg> [accessed 30 May 2022].

AfroMarxist (2009) 'Samora Machel Documentary, 1983' [online] <https://www.youtube.com/watch?app=desktop&v=aRFH1pWDJr0&t=2391s> [accessed 30 May 2022].

Akanbi, A. (2018) 'The problem with wokeness' [online] <https://www.youtube.com/watch?v=_-WimRb2jXs&has_verified=1> [accessed 30 May 2022].

Al Jazeera (2007) 'Frost Over the World - John Kani',22 June [online] <https://www.youtube.com/watch?app=desktop&v=PWYMvfaxDKM> [accessed 24 June 2022].

Arendt, H. (1963) *Eichmann in Jerusalem: A Report on the Banality of Evil*, Penguin, New York.

Australian Government (2008) 'Apology to the Stolen Generations', 13 February [video] <https://www.aph.gov.au/Visit_Parliament/Art/Exhibitions/Custom_Media/Apology_to_Australias_Indigenous_Peoples> [accessed 30 May 2022].

Bakhtin, M. (1984) *Rabelais and His World*, translated by Helene Iswolsky, Indiana University Press, Bloomington.

Baldwin, J. (1963) *The Fire Next Time*, Michael Joseph Publications, London.

Baldwin, J. (1986) 'National Press Club Speech, 12 October 1986' [online] <https://www.youtube.com/watch?v=7_1ZEYgtijk> [accessed 30 May 2022].

Bessette, G. (2004) *Involving the Community: A Guide to Participatory Development Communication*, Southbound, Penang, Malaysia; IDRC, Ottawa.

Billington, M. (2007) 'Nothing But the Truth', 6 February [online] <https://www.theguardian.com/arts/theatre/drama/reviews/story/0,,2006842,00.html> [accessed 30 May 2022].

Boal, A. (1993) *Theatre of the Oppressed*, Theatre Communications Group, New York.

Bogart, A. (2001) *A Director Prepares: Seven Essays on Art and Theatre*, Routledge, London.

Brazile, D. (2019) 'Why I am excited to join Fox News and take part in a civil-and sensible-debate' [online] <https://www.foxnews.com/opinion/donna-brazile-why-i-am-excited-to-join-fox-news-and-take-part-in-a-civil-and-sensible-debate> [accessed 30 May 2022].

Burke, P. (2009) *Popular Culture in Early Modern Europe*, Ashgate, Farnham, UK.

Cadiz, C. and Dagli, W. (2010) 'Adaptive learning: From Isang Bagsak to the ALL in CBNRM Programme', in R.Vernooy (ed.), *Collaborative Learning in Practice: Examples from Natural Resource Management in Asia*, pp. 55–94, Cambridge University Press India, New Delhi; IDRC, Ottawa <https://www.idrc.ca/en/book/collaborative-learning-practice-examples-natural-resource-management-asia> [accessed 30 May 2022].

Cambridge Dictionary (n.d.) 'Empathy' [online] <https://dictionary.cambridge.org/dictionary/english/empathy> [accessed 30 May 2022].

Chambers, R. (1981) 'Poor visibility: How policy makers overlook the poor', *New Internationalist* 96 [online] <https://newint.org/features/1981/02/01/poor-visibility> [accessed 30 May 2022].

Chambers, R. (1994) 'The origins and practice of participatory rural appraisal', *World Development* 22(7): 953–69 <https://doi.org/10.1016/0305-750X(94)90141-4>.

Chimombo, S. (2000) *The Wrath of Napolo*,Wasi Publications, Zomba, Malawi.

Clark, A. (2018) 'Forgiveness has become a forgotten virtue in these bitter times', 20 September [online] <https://www.theguardian.com/comment-isfree/2018/sep/20/forgiveness-forgotten-virtue-bitter-times> [accessed 30 May 2022].

Davis, M. and Troupe, Q. (1989) *Miles: The Autobiography*, Simon & Schuster, New York.

Derrida, J. (1997) *Cosmopolitanism and Forgiveness*, Routledge, London and New York.

Digital Madheads (2015) 'Kanye West's BET Acceptance Speech 2015' [online] <https://www.youtube.com/watch?v=HJYGQ79gBIk> [accessed 24 June 2022].

Djebar, A. (1992) *Women of Algiers in their Apartment*, University of Virginia Press, Charlottesville.

Dubiel, I. (2016) 'Pedagogy of love', *The Huffington Post*, 27 January [online] <https://www.huffpost.com/entry/pedagogy-of-love_b_9078784> [accessed 30 May 2022].

Eade, D. (2007) 'Capacity building: who builds whose capacity'? *Development in Practice* 17: 4–5, 630–639 <https://doi.org/10.1080/09614520701469807>.

Fabian, J. (1990) 'Presence and representation: the other and anthropological writing', *Critical Inquiry* 16(4): 753–772 <https://doi.org/10.1086/448558>.

Fanon, F. (1965) *A Dying Colonialism*, Grove Press, New York.

Flaherty, R. (1922) 'Nanook of the North' [online] <https://www.youtube.com/watch?v=3IAcRjBq93Y> [accessed 30 May 2022].

Frankfurt, H. (1988) *The Importance of What We Care About*, Princeton University Press, Princeton.

Freire, P. (1970) *Pedagogy of the Oppressed*, Bloomsbury, New York.

Freire, P. (1996a) 'An incredible conversation' [online] <https://www.youtube.com/watch?v=aFWjnkFypFA> [accessed 30 May 2022]

Freire, P. (1996b) *Letters to Cristina, Reflections on My Life and Work*, trans. Donaldo Macedo, Quilda Macedo and Alexandre Oliviera, Routledge, London and New York.

Friends of ShaXperience (2014) 'ShakeXperience –Nothing But The Truth', 17 January [online] <https://www.youtube.com/watch?v=gPyrdS1gHo0> [accessed 30 May 2022].

Geertz, C. (1973) *The Interpretation of Cultures: Selected Essays*, Basic Books, New York.

Graham, C. (2017) 'A Howard Government policy that decimated aboriginal communities in 2006 is still reverberating today', *New Matilda*, 23 June [online] <https://newmatilda.com/2017/06/23/bad-aunty-seven-years-how-abc-lateline-sparked-racist-nt-intervention/> [accessed 30 May 2022].

Gramsci, A. (1932) *Selections from Prison Notebooks*, trans. Quintin Hoare and Geoffrey Noelle Smith, International Publishers, New York [online] <https://abahlali.org/files/gramsci.pdf> [accessed 30 May 2022].

Grovier, K. (2019) 'Picasso: The ultimate painter of war?' BBC Art History [online] <https://www.bbc.com/culture/article/20190620-picasso-the-ultimate-painter-of-war> [accessed 30 May 2022].

Gutiérrez, G. (1971) *A Theology of Liberation: History, Politics, and Salvation*, translated by Sister Caridad Inda and John Eaglson, Orbis, Maryknoll, New York.

Hansen, S. (2017) 'Unlearning the myth of American innocence', *The Guardian*, 8 August [online] <https://www.theguardian.com/us-news/2017/aug/08/unlearning-the-myth-of-american-innocence> [accessed 30 May 2022]

Harris, L. (2019) 'Therapy on Stage: Reclaiming Power, Healing Trauma through Theatre and the Expressive Arts' [online] <https://peersnet.org/2019/09/03/therapy-on-stage-reclaiming-power-healing-trauma-through-theater-and-the-expressive-arts/> [accessed 30 May 2022].

Health Communication Capacity Collaborative (2013) *The P-Process: Five Steps to Strategic Communication*, JHU Centre for Communication Programs, Baltimore [online] <http://www.healthcommcapacity.org/wp-content/uploads/2014/04/P-Process-Brochure.pdf> [accessed 30 May 2022].

Higgins, I. and Brennan, B. (2017) 'School attendance, birth weight fell during Northern Territory intervention rollout, study finds', 8 December, ABC News [online] <https://www.abc.net.au/news/2017-12-08/school-attendance-birthweight-fell-during-nt-intervention-study/9238544> [accessed 30 May 2022].

Honan, P. (1998) *Shakespeare: A Life*, Clarendon Press, Oxford.

hooks, b (1991) 'Theory as liberatory practice', *Yale Journal of Law and Feminism* 4(1): 1–13.

hooks, b (1994) *Teaching to Transgress: Education as the Practice of Freedom*, Routledge, New York.

Hurston, Z.H. (1937) *Their Eyes Were Watching God*, Lippincott and Company, Philadelphia.

Kean, D. (2017) 'Chimamanda Ngozi Adichie clarifies transgender comments as backlash grows', *The Guardian*, 13 March [online] <https://www.theguardian.com/books/2017/mar/13/chimamanda-ngozi-adichie-clarifies-transgender-comments> [accessed 30 May 2022].

Khan, T. (2021) 'Racism does not just exist within aid. It is the structure the sector is built on', *The Guardian*, 31 August [online] <https://www.theguardian.com/global-development/2021/aug/31/racism-doesnt-just-exist-within-aid-its-the-structure-the-sector-is-built-on> [accessed 30 May 2022].

Kothari, A., Salleh, A., Escobar, A., Demaria, F., and Acosta, A. (eds) (2019) 'Introduction: finding pluriversal paths', in *Pluriverse: A Post Development Dictionary*, pp. xxi–xl, Tulika Publishing, New Delhi.

Kumar, D. (2014) 'Imperialist feminism and liberalism', Open Democracy [online] <https://www.opendemocracy.net/en/imperialist-feminism-and-liberalism/> [accessed 30 May 2022].

Lammy, D. (2016) 'We need a second referendum. The consequences of Brexit are too grave', *The Guardian*, 26 June [online] <https://www.theguardian.com/politics/commentisfree/2016/jun/26/second-referendum-consequences-brexit-grave> [accessed 30 May 2022].

Lerner, D. (1958) *The Passing of Traditional Society: Modernising the Middle East*, Free Press, New York; Collier-MacMillan, London.

Livingstone, S. (2008) 'On the mediation of everything: ICA Presidential Address 2008', *Journal of Communication* 59(1): 1–18 <https://doi.org/10.1111/j.1460-2466.2008.01401.x>.

Mahmood, S. (2005) *Politics of Piety: The Islamic Revival and the Feminist Subject*, Princeton University Press, Princeton.

Makuwira, J. (2007) 'The politics of community capacity building: contestations, contradictions, tensions and ambivalences in the discourse in indigenous communities in Australia', *The Australian Journal of Indigenous Education* 36: 129–136 <https://doi.org/10.1017/S1326011100004804>.

Makuwira, J. (2014) *Non-Governmental Development Organizations and the Poverty Reduction Agenda: The Moral Crusaders*, Routledge, Oxford and New York.

Malcolm X (1964) 'The Ballot or the Bullet', speech given to the King Solomon Baptist Church in Detroit, 12 April [online] <https://www.youtube.com/watch?v=8zLQLUpNGsc> [accessed30 May 2022].

Malik, N. (2021) 'Vaccine hesitancy is a symptom of people's broken relationship with the state', *The Guardian*, 15 August [online] <https://www.theguardian.com/commentisfree/2021/aug/15/vaccine-hesitancy-broken-relationship-state-conspiracy-theorists> [accessed 30 May 2022].

Mamdani, M. (2007) 'The politics of naming: genocide, civil war, insurgency: Iraq and Darfur', *London Review of Books* (29)5: 5–8 [online] <https://www.lrb.co.uk/the-paper/v29/n05/mahmood-mamdani/the-politics-of-naming-genocide-civil-war-insurgency> [accessed 30 May 2022].

Mansell, R. (2011) 'Whose knowledge counts? A political economy of the knowledge-based society/economy', unpublished presentation, 26 January, IDS Seminar, University of Sussex, Brighton, UK.

Manyozo, L. (2002) 'Community theatre without community participation? Reflections on development support communication programs', *Convergence* 35(4): 55–69.

Manyozo, L. (2017) 'The theory and practice of photo elicitation among the San ≠Khomani of the Southern Kalahari', in N. Wildermuth and T. Ngomba (eds.), *Methodological Reflections on Researching Communication and Social Change*, pp. 79–98, Palgrave Macmillan, Cham.

Manyozo, L., Aliyev, E., Nkhonjera, P., Mauluka, C., and Khangamwa, C. (2020) 'Towards horizontal capacity building: UNICEF Malawi's C4D Learning Labs', in J. Noske-Turner (ed.), *Communication for Development: An Evaluation Framework in Action* (pp. 89–103), Practical Action Publishing, Rugby.

Mao, F. (2018) 'Syphilis: how deadly disease has spread in Australia', BBC News, 26 July [online] <https://www.bbc.com/news/world-australia-44855186> [accessed 30 May 2022].

Martuwarra River of Life, Poelina, A., Bagnall, D., and Lim, M. (2020) 'Recognizing the Martuwarra's First Law Right to Life as a Living Ancestral Being', *Transnational Environmental Law* 9(3): 541–68 <https://doi.org/10.1017/S2047102520000163>.

Marx, K. (1852/2010) *The Eighteenth Brumaire of Louis Bonaparte*, International Publishers, New York.

McCall Smith, A. (2012) *The Limpopo Academy of Private Detection*, Little-Brown, London.

McHugh, S. (2018) 'How two unlikely South Americans transformed an Indigenous art centre', ABC News, 14 May [online] <https://www.abc.net.au/news/2018-05-13/the-outsiders-working-with-indigenous-artists/9704338> [accessed 30 May 2022].

McKenzie, L. (2016) 'Brexit is the only way the working class can change anything', *The Guardian*, 15 June [online] <https://www.theguardian.com/commentisfree/2016/jun/15/brexit-working-class-sick-racist-eu-referendum> [accessed 30 May 2022].

Mellor, D., Bretherton, D., and Firth, L. (2007) 'Aboriginal and non-Aboriginal Australia: the dilemma of apologies, forgiveness, and reconciliation', *Peace and Conflict, Journal of Peace Psychology* 13(1): 11–36 <http://dx.doi.org/10.1080/10781910709336766>.

Mill, J.S. (1859) *On Liberty*, John W. Parker and Son, London.

Mill, J.S. (1859/2017) *The Subjection of Women*, Longmans, Green, Reader and Dyer, London [online] <https://www.earlymoderntexts.com/assets/pdfs/mill1869.pdf> [accessed 30 May 2022].

Mind Tools (2020) 'Empathy at work: developing tools to understand other people' [online] <https://www.mindtools.com/pages/article/EmpathyatWork.htm#:~:text=Cognitive%20empathy%20is%20being%20aware,action%20to%20support%20other%20people.> [accessed 30 May 2022].

Monáe, J. (2018) 'A revolution of love', 18 September [online] <https://www.youtube.com/watch?v=QIz5MHKV1nk> [accessed 30 May 2022].

Morley, C. (2011) 'Joyce Carol Vincent: how could this young woman lie dead and undiscovered for almost three years?' *The Guardian*, 9 October [online] <https://www.theguardian.com/film/2011/oct/09/joyce-vincent-death-mystery-documentary> [accessed 30 May 2022].

Neff, K. (2015) *Self-Compassion: The Proven Power of Being Kind to Yourself*, HarperCollins, New York.

NITV (2017) 'The Intervention', Utopia. Aired on 27 December 2017, 2130–2330.

Nolan, H. (2014) 'A letter from Ray Jasper, who is about to be executed', GAWKER [online] <http:/gawker.com/a-letter-from-ray-jasper-who-is-about-to-be-executed-1536073598> [accessed 30 May 2022].

Northern Territory Government (2007) '"*Ampe Akelyernemane Meke Mekarle*"– Little Children Are Sacred: Report of the Northern Territory Board of Inquiry into the Protection of Aboriginal Children from Sexual Abuse', Northern Territory Government, Darwin [online] <https://apo.org.au/sites/default/files/resource-files/2007-06/apo-nid8402.pdf> [accessed 19 July 2022].

Nsengiyumva, P. (2012) 'Rwanda "gacaca" genocide courts finish work', BBC News, 18 June [online] <https://www.bbc.com/news/world-africa-18490348> [accessed 30 May 2022].

NSW Department of Community Services (2009) *Working with Aboriginal People and Communities: A Practical Guide*, New South Wales Department of Communities, Ashfield [online] <http://www.community.nsw.gov.au/__data/assets/pdf_file/0017/321308/working_with_aboriginal.pdf> [accessed 30 May 2022].

Obolensky, N. (2016) *Complex Adaptive Leadership*, Routledge, Oxford.

Oprah Winfrey Network (2014) 'Dr Maya Angelou on the power of words' [online] <https://www.youtube.com/watch?v=BKv65MdlV-c> [accessed 30 May 2022].

Orwell, G. (1946) 'In front of your nose', *The Tribune*, 22 March [online] <https://www.orwellfoundation.com/the-orwell-foundation/orwell/essays-and-other-works/in-front-of-your-nose/> [accessed 30 May 2022].

Palestine Diary (2012) 'Edward Said on Orientalism' [online] <https://www.youtube.com/watch?v=fVC8EYd_Z_g> [accessed 30 May 2022].

PBS NewsHour (2016) 'This inner-city school is a bridge to empowerment for children of color', 29 December [online] <https://www.youtube.com/watch?v=vHqgm2J8xNk&t=35s> [accessed 30 May 2022].

Post-Crash Economics Society (PCES) (2014) *Economics, Education and Unlearning: Economics Education at the University of Manchester* [online] <https://www.rethinkeconomics.org/wp-content/uploads/2017/03/Economics-Education-and-Unlearning.pdf> [accessed 24 June 2022].

Plato (2004) *Republic*, translated by C.D.C. Reeve, Hackett Publishing Company,Indianapolis.

Progressive Party (1912) 'A Contract with the People: Platform of the Progressive Party', Policy Adopted at the First National Convention, 7 August [online] <https://archives.lib.state.ma.us/bitstream/handle/2452/603940/ocm04756787.pdf?sequence=1&isAllowed=y> [Accessed 18 July 2022].

Psychology Today (n.d.) 'Empathy' [online] <https://www.psychologytoday.com/au/basics/empathy> [accessed 30 May 2022].

Ruby, J. (1991) 'Speaking for, speaking about, speaking with, or speaking alongside: an anthropological and documentary dilemma',*Visual Anthropology Review* 7(2): 50–67.

Rueb, E. and Taylor, D. (2019) 'Obama on call-out culture: that's not activism', *The New York Times*, 31 October [online] <https://www.nytimes.com/2019/10/31/us/politics/obama-woke-cancel-culture.html> [accessed 30 May 2022].

Russell, B. (1935/2004) *In Praise of Idleness*, Routledge, London and Abingdon.

SABC Digital News (2018) 'Stompie Seipei's mother to attend Madikizela-Mandela's Funeral' [online] <https://www.youtube.com/watch?v=GgHSRnM7QCg> [accessed 30 May 2022].

Sachs, W. (2019) 'Foreword: development dictionary revisited', in Kothari, A., Salleh, A., Escobar, A., Demaria, F., and Acosta, A. (eds), *Pluriverse: A Post Development Dictionary*, pp. xi–xvi, Tulika Publishing, New Delhi.

Said, E. (1978) *Orientalism*, Pantheon Books, New York.

Scott, E. (2020) 'Trump says CNN doesn't respect rural Americans: Don Lemon's mocking segment will prove it to them', *The Washington Post*, 29 January [online] <https://www.washingtonpost.com/politics/2020/01/28/trump-said-cnn-doesnt-respect-rural-americans-mocking-segment-will-prove-his-point/> [accessed 16 August 2022].

Shepperd, C. (1981) 'Wisdom from above', *New Internationalist*, 1 February, Issue 96: 7–9.

Silverstone, R. (1999) *Why Study the Media?* Sage, London.

Singh, N. (2017) 'Theatre of trauma', The Theatre School MFA in Directing Theses, 3 [online] <https://via.library.depaul.edu/tts/3> [accessed 30 May 2022].

Spivak, G. (1988) 'Can the subaltern speak?' in N. Cary and L. Grossberg (eds), *Marxism and the Interpretation of Culture* (pp. 271–313), University of Illinois, Chicago.

Stanislavsky, K. (1917) *An Actor Prepares*, translated by Elizabeth Reynolds Hapgood, Eyre Methuen, London.

Stanton, E.C. (1848/2015) *Declaration of Sentiments and Resolutions*, American Roots Publishers, Nashville, TN.

Stoughton, I. (2017) 'Syrian refugee children process trauma through art', *Al Jazeera*, 4 March [online] <https://www.aljazeera.com/features/2017/3/4/syrian-refugee-children-process-trauma-through-art [accessed 30 May 2022].

Taylor, S. (2020) 'Is workplace rudeness on the rise?' *BBC News*, 11 February [online] <https://www.bbc.com/worklife/article/20200207-is-workplace-rudeness-on-the-rise> [accessed 30 May 2022].

The Ellen Show (2018) 'Ellen meets extraordinary New Jersey Principal Akbar Cook',14 September <https://www.youtube.com/watch?v=O1P6oZjfR54> [accessed 24 June 2022].

The Second Vatican Council (1971) *Communio et Progressio: On the Means of Social Communication* [online] <https://www.vatican.va/roman_curia/pontifical_councils/pccs/documents/rc_pc_pccs_doc_23051971_communio_en.html> [accessed 30 May 2022].

The Vatican Council (2020) *Fratelli Tutti - Encyclical Letter of the Holy Father Francis on Fraternity and Social Friendship* [online] <https://www.vatican.va/content/francesco/en/encyclicals/documents/papa-francesco_20201003_enciclica-fratelli-tutti.html> [accessed 30 May 2022].

The View (2018) 'Justice Anthony Kennedy to retire, what's next?' [online] <https:/www.youtube.com/watch?time_continue=148&v=ENPHYygx97g&feature=emb_logo> [accessed 30 May 2022].

Think Nice (2016) 'Bullshit! Featuring Harry Frankfurt' [online] <https:/www.youtube.com/watch?v=_D9Y-1Jcov4&t=1s> [accessed 30 May 2022].

Thompson, E.P. (1963) *The Making of the English Working Class*, Penguin Books, London.

Totenberg, N. and McCammon, S. (2022) 'Supreme Court overturns Roe v. Wade, ending right to abortion upheld for decades' [online] <https://www.npr.org/2022/06/24/1102305878/supreme-court-abortion-roe-v-wade-decision-overturn> [accessed 15 August 2022].

Tutu, D. (2014) 'I am sorry – the three hardest words to say', *The Guardian*, 22 March [online] <https://www.theguardian.com/lifeandstyle/2014/mar/22/archbishop-desmond-tutu-sorry-hard-to-say> [accessed 30 May 2022].

VPRO Metropolis (2014) 'Teaching at a ghetto school in Chicago - VPRO Metropolis',17 February [online] <https:/www.youtube.com/watch?v=D7HcOaPqFUw> [accessed 30 May 2022].

Wa Thiong'o, N. (1977) *Petals of Blood*, Heinemann Publishers, London.

Wa Thiong'o, N. (1986) *Decolonizing the Mind*, Heinemann Publishers, London.

Wainwright, J. (2010) 'On Gramsci's conceptions of the world', *Transactions of the Institute of British Geographers* NS35: 507–21 [online] <https://cpb-us-w2.wpmucdn.com/u.osu.edu/dist/4/45440/files/2017/04/Wainwright-2010-Gramscis-conception-of-the-world-1bh0eu8.pdf> [accessed 30 May 2022].

Ware, C. (2017) 'Time to speak out: the 1980s Australian gay press and personal accounts of living with HIV', *Journal of Australian Studies* 41(4): 472–86 <https://doi.org/10.1080/14443058.2017.1382551>.

Western Australian Museum (2022) 'Tjukurrpa – The dreaming' [online] <https://museum.wa.gov.au/explore/wa-goldfields/first-peoples/tjukurrpa-dreaming> [accessed 30 May 2022].

Wikipedia (n.d.) 'Woke' [online] <https://en.wikipedia.org/wiki/Woke> [accessed 30 May 2022].

Zapatista Movement (1996) 'Fourth Declaration of the Lacandon Jungle: Today we say, we are here, we are rebel dignity, the forgotten of the homeland', 1 January [online] <https://schoolsforchiapas.org/wp-content/uploads/2014/03/Fourth-Declaration-of-the-Lacandona-Jungle-.pdf> [accessed 30 May 2022].

Index

www.ingramcontent.com/pod-product-compliance
Lightning Source LLC
Chambersburg PA
CBHW070630030426
42337CB00020B/3971